Choosing to be Ridiculously Healthy and Unreasonably Happy

How Nobel Prize-winning Telomeres Research and the Looking Good/Feeling Good Tool Can Change Your Life

Greg Brigman, PhD

BALBOA.PRESS

A DIVISION OF HAY HOUSE

Balboa Press books may be ordered through booksellers or by contacting:

Balboa Press
A Division of Hay House
1663 Liberty Drive
Bloomington, IN 47403
www.balboapress.com
1 (877) 407-4847

Because of the dynamic nature of the Internet, any web addresses or links contained in this book may have changed since publication and may no longer be valid. The views expressed in this work are solely those of the author and do not necessarily reflect the views of the publisher, and the publisher hereby disclaims any responsibility for them.

The author of this book does not dispense medical advice or prescribe the use of any technique as a form of treatment for physical, emotional, or medical problems without the advice of a physician, either directly or indirectly. The intent of the author is only to offer information of a general nature to help you in your quest for emotional and spiritual well-being. In the event you use any of the information in this book for yourself, which is your constitutional right, the author and the publisher assume no responsibility for your actions.

Any people depicted in stock imagery provided by Getty Images are models, and such images are being used for illustrative purposes only.
Certain stock imagery © Getty Images.

Print information available on the last page.

ISBN: 978-1-9822-4855-0 (sc)
ISBN: 978-1-9822-4856-7 (e)

Library of Congress Control Number: 2020909747

Balboa Press rev. date: 06/11/2020

CONTENTS

ACKNOWLEDGEMENTS

I want to thank my amazing team who have encouraged and helped to bring this book into being. First to my wife, Dr. Claudia Venable, whose medical background and vast knowledge of nutrition, exercise, love, and happiness, has kept supplying me with new science to check out and incorporate. My daughter, Natalie Silvey, is my visionary, whose kindness and social/emotional intelligence, has been an unwavering support that has kept me going when I hit speed bumps along the way. My sister, Tammy Brewer, whose background in English grammar made her a super editor. To Mikaela Kursell, whose extraordinary work with manuscript preparation was invaluable. And finally, to my mindfulness and yoga friend, who is also an attorney, with an eye for writing, Austin Charles, for his encouragement to put a little more of my personal experience with the ideas in this book front and center. The connecting theme across all of my team is that they live, every day, the lifestyle of ridiculous good health and unreasonable happiness. Thank you all deeply for making this writing journey possible.

INTRODUCTION

Over the last decade, I have been focused on studying the most highly regarded scientific authorities on the topic of optimal living. At the same time, I developed and taught a PhD level course on wellness counseling. This book is a synthesis of the most important ideas I have discovered. I have organized the chapters around a wellness tracking, goal setting, and progress monitoring tool, called "Looking Good/Feeling Good" (LGFG), which I developed and have used for over 20 years. I have personally seen the positive effects of on my energy, mood, aging, and overall wellbeing by monitoring my nutrition, fun/playfulness, exercise, social support, and sleep/rest. I have also used this tool in my university teaching with hundreds of graduate students and have seen consistent positive effects with them. Because I have implemented these powerful ideas into my own life and seen their effects with myself and many others, I believe the ideas in this book to be, not only based on solid science, but also practical wisdom that can help you live your most optimal life. While I am a professor, this book is not purely academic, but rather I designed it to be a practical book to help you apply in your life amazing knowledge and wisdom related to optimal living. My hope is that you will choose the ideas/lessons that best fit your journey to health and happiness.

It was very validating when, in 2009, Dr. Elizabeth Blackburn, a molecular biologist, won the 2009 Nobel Prize in Physiology/Medicine, for her research on protecting the tips of our chromosomes (telomeres). Blackburn's research on telomeres led to the identification of seven factors that protect your telomere length and slow your aging at the cellular level. I was pleased to find that six of the seven factors Blackburn identified are found in my "Looking Good/Feeling Good" wellness-tracking tool. She later teamed up with and Elissa Epel, a psychologist, to write the book, *The Telomere Effect: A Revolutionary Approach to Living Younger, Healthier, and Longer*, which tells the amazing telomere story and how it affects your life and wellbeing. I highly recommend it.

Telomeres are the tips of our chromosomes that protect them. Chromosomes are bundles of tightly coiled DNA located in the nucleus of almost every cell in our body. Cells divide over time, and each time they do, the telomeres are shortened. This process of shortening in your telomeres is associated with aging, cancer, and a higher risk of death. The good news is that we have quite a bit of control over the seven factors that protect your telomers and slow aging that Blackburn at al. (2017) identified.

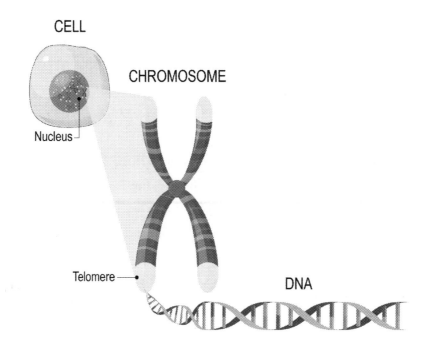

CELL

CHROMOSOME

Nucleus

Telomere

DNA

Seven Factors to Protect Your Telomeres

- Healthy nutrition
- Exercise
- Social Support
- Sleep
- Clinical levels of depression or anxiety
- Exposure to harmful chemicals
- Current major stress exposure (Blackburn at al., 2017)

The LGFG tool incorporates all of Blackburn's seven factors except exposure to harmful chemicals. Please go to this link to download and print your own Looking Good Feeling Good chart https://bit.ly/2AkVuZ1.

LOOKING GOOD / FEELING GOOD

		Week 1	Week 2	Week 3	Week 4	Week 5	Week 6	Week 7	Week 8
1. Nutrition	1	▲▼	▲▼	▲▼	▲▼	▲▼	▲▼	▲▼	▲▼
2. Fun	2	▲▼	▲▼	▲▼	▲▼	▲▼	▲▼	▲▼	▲▼
3. Exercise	3	▲▼	▲▼	▲▼	▲▼	▲▼	▲▼	▲▼	▲▼
4. Social Support	4	▲▼	▲▼	▲▼	▲▼	▲▼	▲▼	▲▼	▲▼
5. Rest	5	▲▼	▲▼	▲▼	▲▼	▲▼	▲▼	▲▼	▲▼
6. Energy	6	▲▼	▲▼	▲▼	▲▼	▲▼	▲▼	▲▼	▲▼
7. Mood	7	▲▼	▲▼	▲▼	▲▼	▲▼	▲▼	▲▼	▲▼

Clinical levels of depression or anxiety are prevented and treated with several of the five items on the LGFG chart. All five of LGFG items are excellent stress-coping strategies and can ameliorate major stress exposure.

The beauty of the LGFG wellness-tracking chart is that it is a simple but powerful tool that allows you to track these five key areas each week and then see how those five ratings affected your mood and energy. We know that even very small positive changes yield significant increases in energy and improvement in mood. When you repeatedly see the direct connection between how you choose to handle your nutrition, fun, exercise, social support, and rest each week, and the effect those choices have on your energy and mood, you become much more aware, and this can lead to your empowerment to change and make healthier choices.

To get started, pick one of the five areas each week that you most want to improve. Then, write a simple but specific plan you think will help you see progress. Next, share your goal and plan with someone who is encouraging about your health and wellness. If possible, recruit one or more of your health buddies to goal-set with you each week. You can do this via email or texting. What we know about habit change is that writing specific goals weekly and monitoring/recording your progress is a key. Add in the social support of friends/family when you share your goals, plans, and successes, and brainstorm new strategies to improve, and you have a strong system to help keep you moving in the right direction of continuous improvement.

Another habit change idea to remember is to be kind to yourself when you do not achieve your goal. Nobody is perfect. When progress is not made, it is important to not doubt your ability. You can and should doubt your strategy or plan. In this case, instead of doubting your ability, you change your strategy. In other words, if what you are doing isn't working, try something different.

Another key to successful behavior change is to look for even very small improvements. We call this the Kaizen approach. Kaizen is a Japanese technique for achieving great and lasting success through small and steady steps. One of the keys to any behavior change is becoming good at noticing even very small improvements. This skill keeps us motivated. We sometimes throw out effective strategies when we do not see large gains quickly, which is counterproductive and undermines our growth. We use a saying to help remind us of this important principle: "Little by little, bit by bit, I'm improving every day." For more on the Kaizen approach, I recommend Robert Maurer's book, *One Small Step Can Change Your Life: The Kaizen Way*.

The next five chapters provide a summary of some of the most compelling research in the areas of nutrition, exercise, fun/play, social support, and rest/sleep. These concise chapters are designed to help you up your health game and reap the reward of higher energy and more positive mood, along with slowing the aging process and boosting your overall wellness.

Chapter 6 provides additional tools for building resilience and managing stress and concludes with a summary of how to get the most joy and happiness from your life. All chapters are built upon the "AH-HA, TA-DA, HAHA" format. If you are not familiar that means: AH-HAs = new ideas to help you grow in health and wellness; the TA-DAs = giving yourself credit for many healthy lifestyle choices you have made (and continue to make); and HAHA = looking for the humor, laughter, lightness, and fun of a situation, including reading, discussing, and applying this book to your lifestyle.

References

Blackburn, E., & Epel, E. (2017). *The telomere effect: A revolutionary approach to living younger, healthier, longer*. Grand Central Publishing.

Brigman, G., Villares, E., & Webb, L. (2018). *Looking good/feeling good* [Infographic]. Evidence-based school counseling: A student success approach. Routledge.

Maurer, R. (2014). *One small step can change your life: The Kaizen way.* Workman Publishing Company.

Nobel Foundation. (2009). *Elizabeth H. Blackburn, Carol W. Greider, Jack W. Szostak: The Nobel Prize in Physiology or Medicine 2009.* https://www.nobelprize.org/prizes/medicine/2009/press-release/

Pang, S. (2012). *A review of potential analytical approaches for detecting cloned animals and their offspring in the food chain* [Clip art]. https://assets.publishing.service.gov.uk/government/uploads/system/uploads/attachment_data/file/332618/Cloned_animal_report.pdf

CHAPTER 1

NUTRITION

"The secret of life is enjoying the passage of time"
—James Taylor, "The Secret of Life"

Chapter Highlights:

- Michael Pollan's *Food Rules*
- David Katz - Prevention Research Center, Yale School of Medicine
- U.S. News & World Report on "Best Diets"
- National Institutes of Health (NIH) Guidelines
- U.S. Department of Agriculture (USDA) Guidelines
- Inflammation
- Pilar Gerasimo's "Top 7 Suggestions for Healthy, Conscious Eating"

LOOKING GOOD / FEELING GOOD

1. Nutrition
Liquids: ▲ water & milk & juice ▼ sodas
Solids: ▲ fruits & veggies ▼ sweets & chips

	Week 1	Week 2	Week 3	Week 4	Week 5	Week 6	Week 7	Week 8
1	▲▼	▲▼	▲▼	▲▼	▲▼	▲▼	▲▼	▲▼

Think about your week.
Circle the up triangle if you improved even a little this past week.

For example: Did you eat even a little more fruit or vegetables?
Did you eat even a little less sweets or chips?
Did you drink even a little more water or a little less soda?

There is a lot of information and science on what to eat and not eat, and much of it is contradictory. So, what is one to believe? What is the best diet for health and longevity?

Maybe there is not just one diet that is best for everyone. Consider that many traditional diets around the world yield populations that live long healthy lifetimes. When looking at these traditional diets, you should be aware that most of these populations also are much more active than most modern western populations.

There is also a new diet almost every few months vying for our attention and making claims to be the new healthy way to eat. Selling the next new diet fad is a big business with big advertising bucks trying to convince us that they have a lock on some new information that makes their new diet special and better. While this can be very confusing, there is massive agreement within the medical and scientific community, which researches nutrition, on what is the healthiest way to eat. So, if we look at the solid science about what to eat to stay healthy, we find it is not confusing; it is straight forward and pretty simple. Here are a half-dozen sources that summarize the latest science on healthy nutrition. I suggest you look for commonalities from this range of authoritative sources. As you do, you will gain confidence in your knowledge and ability to make good nutrition choices that help you stay healthy.

I start by looking at science writer Michael Pollan's (2019) *Food Rules: An Eater's Manual.* He lays out an impressive amount of research in easy to understand language. He makes it clear what not to eat. He summarizes his research review in seven words: "Eat food, not too much and mostly plants" (Pollan, 2009). Pollan's (2009) "3 FACTS" are quite compelling:

FACT #1
Populations that eat the so-called Western diet generally defined as consisting of processed foods and meats, lots of added fat and sugar, lots of refined grains, lots of everything except vegetables and whole grains—invariably suffer from high rates of obesity and type 2 diabetes, cardiovascular disease, and cancer. Virtually all of obesity and type 2 diabetes, 80% of cardiovascular disease, and more than a third of all cancers can be linked to this diet. (Pollan, 2009)

FACT #2
Populations eating a remarkably wide range of traditional diets generally don't suffer from these chronic diseases. These diets run the gamut from ones very high in fat

(the Inuit in Greenland subsist largely on seal blubber) to ones high in carbohydrates (Central American Indians subsist largely on maize and beans) to ones very high in protein (Masai tribesmen in Africa subsist chiefly on cattle blood, meat, and milk). (Pollan, 2009)

FACT #3

People who get off the Western diets and lifestyle see dramatic improvements in their health. A study published in *Nutritional Genomics: Discovering the Path to Personalized Nutrition*, Eds. Jim Kaput and Raymond Rodriquez (New York: John Wiley & Sons, 2006) showed that when a typical American population departed from the Western diet (and lifestyle) they can reduce chances of getting coronary heart disease by 80%, type 2 diabetes by 90% and colon cancer by 70%. The diet consisted of low trans fats, high ratio of polyunsaturated fats to saturated fats, a high whole-grain intake, two serving of fish a week, the recommended daily allowance of folic acid and at least 5 grams of alcohol a day. The lifestyle changes included not smoking, maintaining a body mass index (BMI) below 25, and 30 minutes a day of exercise. (Pollan, 2009)

This is consistent with the research on people living in the so-called "Blue Zones," areas across the world where people typically live to be 100. Across these zones we find the people eat mostly plants, don't smoke, are physically active, sleep well, are not stressed out, and have strong social ties. Sounds a lot like the "Looking Good/Feeling Good" (LGFG) tool we are using and organizing this book around. Pollan's (2009) "3 FACTS" make the case that changing our diet and lifestyle to a healthier one leads to significant gains in health.

My next source on nutrition science is David Katz, MD, Director of the Prevention Research Center at Yale University School of Medicine, Past-President of the American College of Lifestyle Medicine, and Founder and President of the True Health Initiative. Dr. Katz is probably the most widely respected authority on the science behind healthy nutrition. He has over 200 published articles and 16 books on the subject. His passion is to educate people about healthy eating.

Try googling "True Health Initiative" for another rich source of nutrition science. I also highly recommend that you take a look online at "Nutrition Rounds Podcast," hosted by Dr. Danielle Belardo, MD, featuring Dr. Katz (Episode 1, June 2019). In this interview, Katz emphasizes that the food industry, big PHARMA, and the nutrition-book industry have done a really good job in bamboozling Americans about nutrition because they make money by selling what's new and exciting (Belardo, 2019), while the truth is, we already know through decades of research how to eat healthy. Lastly, David Katz's (2018) book, *The Truth About Food*, is an incredible resource on the latest science on nutrition.

According to Katz (2018), 80% of premature death is caused by lifestyle practices. He cites the seminal *JAMA* article, "Actual Causes of Death in the United States," by McGinnis and Foege (1993), where they lay out 10 factors that cause most premature deaths. The top 3 causes in 1993 were smoking, diet, and lack of physical activity (McGinnis & Foege, 1993). Katz says that in 2019, diet took the #1 spot as a cause of premature death. His research and reviews of research confirm much of what Pollan recommended just before, and what you will find just after this section (from U.S. News & World Report, NIH, and USDA guidelines). The recommendations can be summed up with this quote:

> Eat Like a Greek to Prevent Disease. Want to live longer, slim down, and lower your risk of heart disease, cancer, diabetes, and dementia? Adopting a Mediterranean diet full of whole grains, legumes, fruits and vegetables, lean protein, and unsaturated fats (e.g., olive oil) can help get you there. When you eat a diet that's good for the heart, you're doing your brain, liver, immune system, and every other system the same favor. (Katz, 2018)

In a March 2020 Wall Street Journal article by Bittman and Katz (2020), authors of *How to Eat: All Your Food and Diet Questions Answered*, good diets are summed up this way: "the truth is that all good diets feature one or another balanced assemblage of wholesome, real foods-mostly plants." In their book, the authors say two major themes cut across a host of research summaries: minimally processed food and plant predominant diets are healthiest. They conclude that the recently popular Keto diet is really the Atkins diet, which features high protein, low carbohydrates, and is not a sustainable healthy approach. Similarly, the authors are not fans of the Paleo diet for two reasons. First, the paleo hunter-gatherer was tremendously active, unlike most modern people. Secondly, the meat they ate was approximately 7% fat, as compared to the 35% fat of meat today.

Here is Bittman and Katz's (2020) take on the research on several foods many people have questions about:

Beans: The authors debunk the theory that lectins in beans might be bad for you and conclude that we have known for some time, based on massive evidence, that people who eat beans and legumes routinely had better health not worse than people who did not. Beans are one of the most common foods in the world's "Blue Zones," where people routinely live to 100.

Meat: Whether eating meat is good or bad for you depends on the kind of meat you are talking about. If the meat comes from grain-fed cattle, then nearly 35% of the calories come from fat, much of it saturated. By contrast, grass-fed beef, chicken, and lean turkey each provide incremental improvement.

Dairy: Whether milk products are good or bad for you depend on several factors, including what dairy it comes from, your metabolism, your genes and what it replaces in your diet. Dairy can provide health benefits, but an optimal diet doesn't require dairy.

Fish: Salmon and other fish rich in omega-3 fatty acids are good if they replace red and processed meat.

> "Nutrition may be one of the most neglected inhibitors of disabling stress.
> The general principles of good nutrition maybe easily violated under pressure.
> Staying in tune with your body is especially important at such times"
> —Kenneth Matheny and Richard Riordan, *Stress and Strategies of Lifestyle Management*

Next, is a summary of science around healthiest diets which is done annually by U.S. News & World Report. Katz was one of the experts conducting the review. Both Pollan and Katz have called for eating what amounts to some variation of the Mediterranean diet.

So, it should not be a surprise that the U.S. News & World Report (2015) review of the science around nutrition found that the Mediterranean diet is the best diet for the following categories:

- Overall
- Heart Health
- Healthy Eating
- Easy to Follow

- Nutrition
- Safety
- Best Plant-Based Diets

Let's take a look at what makes up the Mediterranean diet. Does this list look familiar?

- Whole grains
- Vegetables
- Fruits
- Olive Oil
- Nuts, Beans
- Cheese, Yogurt
- Fish, Shellfish
- Eggs
- Meats in small portions
- Water
- Wine in moderation

In a more recent January 2, 2019 publication, for the second year in a row, the Mediterranean diet was named the best diet in America by *U.S. News & World Report.* According to Ducharme (2019):

> Following a Mediterranean diet involves eating lots of plants, whole grains, healthy fats (such as olive oil) and lean proteins, and cutting back on processed foods, red meat and refined sugars. The diet has long been linked to many health benefits, including lower risks of cancer and heart disease, better kidney health and a healthier gut.

In the U.S. News & World Report's latest rankings, the Mediterranean diet also took the titles of "Best Diet" for healthy eating, diabetes, heart health; the "Easiest Diet to Follow"; and the "Best Plant-based Diet."

While no single diet is best for everyone, *U.S. News'* expert rankings are meant to promote the eating styles most likely to improve health and steer people away from misguided diet plans— like the last-place Dukan diet, a restrictive, high-protein system.

Now, let's compare Pollan's, Katz's and U.S. News & World Report's findings with the latest guidelines from the National Institutes of Health (NIH). Spoiler alert, you will see lots of agreement. According to NIH guidelines:

> The way to achieve a healthy body weight is to balance energy intake (food and drink) with energy used (physical activity). The healthiest way to reduce calories is to reduce intake of added sugars, saturated and trans fats, and alcohol, which provide a lot of calories but few or no essential nutrients. Calorie intake can also be reduced by decreasing the size of food portions and limiting the intake of foods and drinks that are high in calories, fat, and/or refined sugars, and which provide few nutrients. (National Institutes of Health, n.d.)

NIH's examples of foods to limit or avoid include fried food, cookies, cakes, candy, ice cream, and sweetened soft drinks. The NIH guidelines also include more specific targets for our nutritional health such as:

Eat 5 or more servings of vegetables and fruits each day.
- Include vegetables and fruits at every meal and for snacks.

Choose whole grains over processed (refined) grains and sugars.
- Choose whole grain rice, bread, pasta, and cereals.

Limit intake of processed meats and red meats.
- Choose fish, poultry, or beans instead of beef, pork, and lamb.

If you drink alcoholic beverages, limit your intake.
- No more than 2 drinks per day for men and 1 drink a day for women. (National Institutes of Health, n.d.)

We would expect similar guidance on diet from the U.S. Department of Agriculture (USDA) "Dietary Guidelines for Americans 2015–2020." The USDA (2015) guideline's summary does indeed offer very similar advice and more specifics, which are summarized here under three headings:

1. **Follow a healthy eating pattern across the lifespan.** A healthy eating pattern includes:
   - A variety of vegetables from all subgroups—dark green, red and orange, legumes (beans and peas), starchy, and other
   - Fruits, especially whole fruits
   - Grains, at least half of which are whole grains
   - Fat-free or low-fat dairy, including milk, yogurt, cheese, and/or fortified soy beverages
   - A variety of protein foods, including seafood, lean meats and poultry, eggs, legumes (beans and peas), and nuts, seeds, and soy products
   - Oils
2. **Focus on variety, nutrient density, and amount.**
3. **Limit calories from added sugars and saturated fats and reduce sodium intake.**

So far, the five sources above have been fairly consistent with their nutrition guidelines for health. Next, I want to tie what we eat to another major cause of disease: inflammation.

Inflammation Causes or Is a Contributor to Virtually Every Major Disease

The Rancho Bernardo Study (RBS) of Healthy Aging, a 25-year study of older Californians, found that the higher your Interleukin ([IL-6]—associated with inflammation) levels, the earlier you die. Fat, especially belly fat is not your friend. It is where lots of inflammation is created. Here are some guidelines for reducing fat and inflammation:

- Cut out fried foods, fast foods, sugary drinks
- Cut back on carbs and replace with veggies and fruit
- Shoot for a moderate amount of lean protein (not high protein diet).

For a detailed list of foods that can reduce inflammation, take a look at Dr. Andrew Weil's anti-inflammatory diet: *https://www.drweil.com/wp-content/uploads/2017/06/dr-weils-anti-inflammatory-diet-and-food-pyramid-print.pdf*

I want to end this chapter on nutrition by sharing some encouraging facts about how your nutrition can change your body at the cellular level and some tips for conscious eating.

Rebuild Your Body at the Cellular Level

The average human body is composed of fifty to seventy-five trillion cells. All of those cells, including your one hundred billion nerve cells, are completely reconstructed more than twice a year. What you eat and drink provides the fuel for this cellular renewal. Therefore, we all have the ability to rebuild our bodies from the cellular level each year, and the foods we eat are the building blocks for that yearly reconstruction. So, take a moment, and reflect on the questions below.

1. What are some of the healthy foods you already eat?
2. What are a few healthy foods you want to add to your diet?
3. What are a few of the foods you want to cut back on or eliminate to be healthier?

This chapter has focused on "What" to eat. I want to end with some notes from Pilar Gerasimo, one of my favorite wellness authors, on "How" to eat consciously. Gerasimo is a former editor of *Experience Life* magazine and author of "A Manifesto for Thriving in a Mixed-Up World." She has a weekly wellness podcast, *The Living Experiment.* You can find more about her work at: www.pilargerasimo.com

Seven of Pilar's Top Suggestions for Healthy, Conscious Eating

1. **Focus**: Eliminate screens—no smart phones, computers, TV or iPads. Skip books, newspapers, and magazines. Use mealtimes as a break from work and multi-tasking.
2. **Slow down**: Consciously tell yourself that mealtime is for relaxing, chilling. Put your fork down between bites.

3. **Sit tall and still**: Tell your nervous system and digestive system to relax by using this position, instead of sitting in the "Go" position of hunching over, head lowered to food. Sit up, keep feet flat on floor, and notice how different it feels from the "Go" position.

4. **Breathe**: Take some deep breaths before you begin eating and continue to breathe deeply through your nose as you eat. Many people unconsciously hold their breath while eating, which sends a stress response message rather than a relax message to the nervous system.

5. **Take small bites**: Aim for manageable amounts. Taking large bites makes chewing harder and inclines you to swallow larger quantities of food without fully tasting them.

6. **Chew**: Keep chewing more than you think you need, until your food is in a smooth, liquid state. This will improve your digestion and decrease overeating.

7. **Enjoy**: Savor the experience of slowing down, smelling the aromas, appreciating the appearance and flavor of your food. Eat with love and appreciation for your food, for yourself and for your dining companions.

Conclusion

The evidence seems strong that highly processed, high sugar, and high carbohydrate foods are not our friends. It also seems pretty clear that eating a variety of vegetables, fruits, and lean protein will keep us healthier and allow us to live longer. So, use your Look Good/Feeling Good (LFGF) wellness-tracking chart to monitor your progress on your nutrition, as well as on the other four factors. Remember that all five LGFG factors—nutrition, fun, exercise, social support, and rest/sleep—interact with one another, and all contribute to how much energy you have and how you feel. So, set some reasonable nutrition goals for yourself, and remember the Kaizen principal of improving little-by-little each day. Good luck in improving your daily diet and experiencing the health gains as you do.

References

Belardo, Danielle. (Host). (2019). Episode 1–David Katz MD (No. 1) [Audio podcast episode]. In *Nutrition rounds podcast*. Nutrition Rounds. https://nutritionrounds.libsyn.com/ episode-1-david-katz-md

Bittman, M., & Katz, D. (2020). *How to eat: All your food and diet questions answered.* Houghton Mifflin Harcourt.

Bittman, M., & Katz, D. (2020, March 7). We actually know what we should eat. *The Wall Street Journal.* https://www.wsj.com/articles/we-actually-know-what-we-should-eat-11583540287

Brigman, G., Villares, E., & Webb, L. (2018). *Looking good/feeling good* [Infographic]. Evidence-based school counseling: A student success approach. Routledge.

Ducharme, J. (2019). These are the 5 best diets for 2019, according to experts. *Time.* https://time.com/5486616/best-diet-mediterranean-diet/

Gerasimo, P. (2020). *Pilar Gerasimo.* https://pilargerasimo.com/

Kaput, J., & Rodriguez, R. (Eds.). (2006). *Nutritional genomics: Discovering the path to personalized nutrition.* Wiley.

Katz, D. (n.d.). *Creating a world free of preventable disease: A global consensus of lifestyle as medicine.* True Health Initiative. https://www.truehealthinitiative.org/

Katz, D. (2018). *The truth about food: Why pandas eat bamboo and people get bamboozled.* Independently published.

Matheny, K., & Riordan, R. (1992). *Stress and strategies for lifestyle management.* Georgia State University Press.

McGinnis, J., & Foege, W. (1993). Actual causes of death in the United States. *JAMA, 270*(18), 2207–12.

National Institutes of Health. (n.d.). *National Institutes of Health: Turning discover into health.* https://www.nih.gov/

Pollan, M. (2009). *Food rules: An Eater's Manual.* Penguin Books.

Taylor, J. (1977). Secret of Life [Song]. On *JT.* Columbia Records.

University of California, San Diego. (n.d.). *The Rancho Bernardo Study of Healthy Aging.* https://knit.ucsd.edu/ranchobernardostudy/

U.S. Department of Health & Human Services and U.S. Department of Agriculture. (2015). *Dietary guidelines for Americans 2015–2020* (8th ed). https://health.gov/sites/default/files/2019-09/2015-2020_Dietary_Guidelines.pdf

U.S. News & World Report. (2015, January 6). U.S. News & World Report announces Best Diets of 2015. *U.S. News & World Report.* https://www.usnews.com/info/blogs/press-room/2015/01/06/us-news-announces-best-diets-of-2015

U.S. News & World Report. (2019). Best diets. *U.S. News & World Report.* https://health.usnews.com/best-diet

U.S. News & World Report. (2019, January 2). U.S. News reveals Best Diet Rankings for 2019. *U.S. News & World Report.* https://www.usnews.com/info/blogs/press-room/articles/2019-01-02/us-news-reveals-best-diets-rankings-for-2019

Weil Lifestyle, LLC. (2017). *Dr. Weil's anti-inflammatory diet and food pyramid.* https://cdn.drweil.com/wp-content/uploads/2017/06/dr-weils-anti-inflammatory-diet-and-food-pyramid-print.pdf

CHAPTER 2

FUN—HOORAY FOR THE POWER OF PLAY

"The secret of genius is to carry the spirit of the child into old age"
—Aldous Huxley

Chapter Highlights:

- Ashley Montagu - *Growing Young*
- Ten Neoteny Traits
- Stuart Brown - *Play: How it Shapes the Brain, Opens the Imagination, and Invigorates the Soul*
- "Certificate of Playfulness"
- "20 Things That Bring You Joy"
- "How Much Joy, Peace, and Happiness Can You Tolerate?"

LOOKING GOOD / FEELING GOOD

2. Fun
Little joys, big fun - it all counts, read, listen to music, play, create, hangout, explore

	Week 1	Week 2	Week 3	Week 4	Week 5	Week 6	Week 7	Week 8
2	▲▼	▲▼	▲▼	▲▼	▲▼	▲▼	▲▼	▲▼

Think about your week.
Circle the up triangle if you improved even a little this past week.

For example: Did you spend even a little more time doing any of the things you enjoy this week?

This chapter will attempt to convince you that we all need to take fun and play seriously. Fun and play are essential to health and stress management and are especially important to creativity, innovative thinking, problem-solving, and relationships. Think of fun and play as essential in your ability to adapt to change.

One of my favorite books is *Growing Young* by Ashley Montagu, an anthropologist at Rutgers University. He explains the concept of "neoteny" which I think you will find fascinating.

In his newer, revised edition, Montagu (1988) encourages us to reevaluate the way we think about growth and development: "Humans are designed to grow and develop their childlike qualities, and not to become the ossified adults prescribed by society" (p. 104).

Montagu explains how our culture, schools, and families frequently work against our keeping important childlike traits which we need for both physical and mental growth, such as the need to love; to learn, wonder, and know; to explore, think, and experiment; to be imaginative, creative, and curious; and to sing, dance, and play. He shows us how to prevent psycho-sclerosis. One of my favorite Montagu quotes is: "The goal of life is to die young, as old as possible."

In the "Preface" to *Growing Young*, Montagu notes that Stephen Jay Gould of Harvard University—a paleontologist, evolutionary biologist, and historian of science—calls the quote above, "The best statement ever written on the most important, neglected theme of human life and evolution" (as cited in Montagu, 1988, p. ix). So, let's look at what Montagu means when he talks about neoteny and growing young.

Neoteny: The Spirit of the Child

Traits of childhood behavior that are so valuable and that tend to disappear gradually as human beings grow older include: curiosity, imaginativeness, playfulness, open mindedness, willingness to experiment, flexibility, humor, energy, receptiveness to new ideas, and perhaps the most valuable of all, the need to love. According to Montagu (1988), all normal children, unless their elders have corrupted them, show these qualities every day of their childhood years. Life at any level of social development is a pretty complex business, and it is met and handled most efficiently by those exhibiting the greatest capacity for adaptability—*plasticity*—the supremely neotenous trait of humans. It is the need to love others and to be loved, and the qualities of inquisitiveness, thirst for knowledge, need to learn, imagination, creativity, sense of humor, joy, optimism, honesty, resilience, and compassionate intelligence, which constitute the spirit of the child.

Another great contributor to the notion of the importance of nurturing our childlike traits, including imagination, is Edith Cobb, who wrote the seminal book, *The Ecology of Imagination in Childhood*. Young (1988) provides a description of Cobb's work:

> As a result of twenty years of research, including extensive fieldwork, Edith Cobb concluded that a major clue to mental as well as psychological and psychophysical health lies in the spontaneous and innately creative imagination of childhood. (p. 131)

Imagination is the power of forming mental images of what is not actually present. The child's "let's pretend," is similar to the scientist's "as if." The scientist says: "Let me treat this *as if* it worked this way, and we will see what happens." The highest praise one can bestow upon a scientist is that he or she is a person of great imagination.

First published as a book in 1977, *The Ecology of Imagination in Childhood*, Cobb's collection of autobiographies and biographies of creative people, as well as her observations of children's play, suggests that genius is shaped by the imagination of childhood. She sees the child as innately connected with the natural world. Her book remains an important philosophical meditation on the importance of children's deep experience with nature to their adult cognition and psychological well-being.

Take a moment and rate yourself on these ten neoteny traits. Then, place a star beside the 2–3 you are most proud of and a checkmark beside the 2–3 you most want to increase. Share your rating with a friend and enjoy the conversation that follows.

Ten Neoteny Traits

1. curiosity	1	2	3	4	5
2. imaginativeness	1	2	3	4	5
3. playfulness	1	2	3	4	5
4. open mindedness	1	2	3	4	5
5. willingness to experiment	1	2	3	4	5
6. flexibility	1	2	3	4	5
7. humor	1	2	3	4	5
8. energy	1	2	3	4	5
9. joy	1	2	3	4	5
10. optimism	1	2	3	4	5

Another favorite resource of mine is Stuart Brown's book on play.

Stuart Brown, MD, is a psychiatrist and co-author of *Play: How it Shapes the Brain, Opens the Imagination, and Invigorates the Soul.* He makes quite a strong case for the importance of play as we age. As adults, the primary purpose of play is to get us back in touch with the joy we have all had at some point in our lives.

Brown also researched play in the animal kingdom, with the support of National Geographic and Jane Goodall. Through his observations and discussions with animal play experts from around the world, he concluded that play was an evolved behavior in animals, necessary for survival, and a developmentally important human process. He finds that free play develops the social and locomotive skills in children that are necessary later in life for creative thinking.

In 2006, Brown founded the National Institute for Play to further research and to bring the benefits of play to the general public. Brown has conducted over 6,000 interviews with diverse groups of people, including Nobel Prize winners, CEOs, and serial murderers, to obtain their play histories. His evaluation of these led him to conclude that play is very important in people's lives and the effects of play-deprivation is quite striking. According to Brown (2010), "The ability of play is critical not only to being happy, but also to sustaining social relationships and being a creative, innovative person."

Brown has been on a mission to get the word out on the power of play. He has presented on Ted Talks and on a PBS special, "The Promise of Play." Additionally, he is the founder of the National Institute of Play and helped create the *American Journal of Play*.

Brown (2010) promotes the following three benefits of making play a priority:

- Play shapes the brain and makes us smarter and more adaptable.
- Play fosters empathy and makes possible complex social groups.
- Play lies at the core of creativity and innovation.

So, what is play? Play is defined as apparently purposeless, voluntary, inherently attractive, free-from-time, and improvisational, with diminished self-consciousness. Brown (2010) ends *Play* with seven suggestions for bringing play into our lives.

1. Take your play history. Remembering what brought you joy gets you at least halfway home to learning how to create it again in your present life.
2. Expose yourself to play. Joy, humor, fun, are all around us, if we allow ourselves to see them.
3. Give yourself permission to be playful, to be a beginner. Get over looking silly, undignified, or dumb.
4. Fun is your North Star, but you don't always have to head north. What's fun for one person may not be fun at all for the next. We have to be attuned with what brings us joy.
5. Be active. Doing something physical is one of the quickest ways to bring play into your life. Just move.
6. Free yourself from fear. Fear and play do not go together. Find your own special place where you can feel free, relaxed, at ease and uninhibited.
7. Nourish your mode of play and be with people who nourish it too. Find the play that feeds your soul. Make a commitment to stay play nourished.

So now that your appetite for increasing your fun and play have been whetted, I invite you to take a playful walk through the following certification process.

> "Play helps you regain the mind of a child and better
> deal with the major problems and challenges we all face"
> —Bowen White, MD, pioneer in stress medicine

Certificate of Playfulness

Is a lifetime member and in good standing with the
Growing Young Society

You are hereby and forever entitled to:

Walk in the rain, chase after rainbows, smell flowers, blow bubbles, stop along the way, build sandcastles, watch the moon & stars rise, smile at strangers, go barefoot, sing in the shower, read children books, take bubble baths, have a merry heart, hold hands, hug and kiss, fly kites, laugh and cry for the health of it, wander around, feel scared, sad, mad, happy, give up worry and guilt & shame, stay innocent, say yes, say no, say magic words, ask lots of questions, ride bicycles, draw and paint, see things differently, talk with animals, climb trees, take naps, do nothing, daydream, play with toys, learn new stuff, listen to music, tell stories, make a new friend, celebrate a sunset, feel the morning dew on grass, call an old friend, examine a leaf, laugh at a comedy club, shower together soaping each other's backs, take deep breaths, brush someone's hair, give a massage, get a massage, behold a vista, savor a new food, plant a garden, skip stones in a pond, feed ducks, spoon with your love, listen to children's laughter, give a gift for no reason, feel waves lapping at your feet, pay someone a compliment, think wondrous thoughts, do more of what brings you joy, happiness, abundance, grace, courage, balance, spontaneity, passion, peace and life energy.

You are encouraged to always remember the motto of the
Growing Young Society:

"The goal in life is to die young. As old as possible."

20 Things That Bring You Joy

One tool that helps you to identify and be more aware of activities that spark joy, increase your fun, and engage you in play, is "20 Things That Bring You Joy." What I have found is that it takes a little time to get past your first 5–10 activities. However, there is a payoff for identifying the next ten to get to at least 20 activities that are fun for you and bring you joy. After you list the 20 activities, use the check boxes across the top to determine whether you usually do each activity alone or with others, whether it costs $10 or more each time you do it (note some activities cost more for equipment to get started, such as tennis, but may not cost each time you engage in it). The other categories to check are whether you usually do this activity inside or outside, and whether you have recently participated in this activity. What I find helpful about doing this practice is that you may surprise yourself by having more fun with a ready-made list you can use when you feel bored or in need of a "play pick me up." Some post this list in a spot where they see it often to remind themselves that there are almost always activities they can do to spark joy. Once you complete your "Joy Activity Grid," reflect on these open questions:

- What were you most pleased about?
- What surprised you?
- What are your most important takeaways?
- What do you see that you need to do?

20 Things That Bring You Joy

List things that you find joy in doing. These can be simple or complex, cost money or not.
Involve others or done solo. The only criteria is that when you engage in them they routinely
make your feel joyful and happy. For each section list 2-3 specific things.

Activity	Alone	Others	$	Outside	Inside	W/I Week	W?I Month	

Pick 2 you most want to do within the next week:

Write a plan to do these. Include day and time and any needed details.

Share with a partner and let your enthusiasm show.

How much joy, peace, & happiness can you tolerate?

Have you ever noticed yourself or others start to look for the negative when things are going well? Sometimes in sports you hear about athletes not accepting victory and somehow finding a way to lose. For example, the golfer who is shooting very well, actually better than usual and then starts to loose their swing, their rhythm their concentration and the bad shots start to show up.

It is as though we cannot stand for things to go so well. We may have an unconscious set point above which we cannot accept things going well and begin to manufacture failure or disappointment.

What if you could change that mechanism? What if your new mantra was "things are going great, and I could stand for them to be even better?"

This could be an important decision for you. You could reset your joy button to a much higher level. It takes conscious choice. But be aware, if you start to develop more than three of the symptoms listed below you could be headed for serious inner peace.

Symptoms of Inner Peace (SIP)

- **Tendency to think and act spontaneously rather than from fears based on past experiences.**
- **An unmistakable ability to enjoy each moment.**
- **Loss of interest in judging self or others.**
- **Loss of interest in conflict.**
- **Loss of the ability to worry. (Note, this is a very serious symptom).**
- **Frequent, overwhelming episodes of appreciation.**
- **Contented feelings of connectedness with others and nature.**
- **Frequent attacks of smiling through the eyes of the heart**
- **Increasing susceptibility to love extended by others, as well as the uncontrollable urge to extend love to others.**
- **Increasing tendency to let things happen, rather than to make them happen.**

   Dr. Jeff Rockwell warns: "If you have all or even most of the above symptoms, please be advised that the condition of inner peace may be so far advanced as to not be treatable".

   If these symptoms continue for more than one month, you may develop a full blown inner peace disorder (IPD).

References

Bowen, W. (2004). *Why normal isn't healthy: How to find heart, meaning, passion, & humor on the road most traveled* (2nd ed.). Stress Technologies.

Brigman, G., Villares, E., & Webb, L. (2018). *Looking good/feeling good* [Infographic]. Evidence-based school counseling: A student success approach. Routledge.

Brown, S. (2010). *Play: How it shapes the brain, opens the imagination, and invigorates the soul*. Avery.

Cobb, E. (1959). The ecology of imagination in childhood. *Daedalus, 88*(3), 537–548. www.jstor.org/stable/20026521.

Cobb, E. (1977). *The ecology of imagination in childhood*. Columbia University Press.

Montagu, A. (1981). *Growing young*. McGraw-Hill.

Montagu, A. (1988). *Growing young* (2nd ed.). Praeger.

Quotes.net. (n.d.) *Aldous Huxley*. Retrieved April 29, 2020, from https://www.quotes.net/quote/5897

Siegel, B. (1990). *Peace, love and healing: Body mind communication & the path to self-healing: An exploration*. Quill.

CHAPTER 3

EXERCISE—THE NEW MIRACLE CURE

"Physical activity is crucial to the way we think and feel"
—John Ratey, MD, *Spark: The Revolutionary New Science of Exercise and the Brain*

Chapter Highlights:

- Six Reasons to Exercise: Which Ones Are Most Important to You?
- Stay Fit, Stay Young, Stay Energized: The Role of Exercise and Mitochondria
- Exercise, Your Cardio Health, and Maximum Oxygen Uptake (VO2 Max)
- *Spark: The Revolutionary New Science of Exercise and the Brain*
- Exercise Guidelines from NIH, CDC, and AHA
- "Exercise: The Miracle Cure," The Academy of Medical Royal Colleges
- The Right Dose of Exercise
- Exercise and Brain Functioning
- *Spring Chicken: Stay Young Forever or Die Trying*

LOOKING GOOD / FEELING GOOD

		Week 1	Week 2	Week 3	Week 4	Week 5	Week 6	Week 7	Week 8
3. Exercise Walk, run, dance, pedal, move it - 30 minutes or more a day	3	▲▼	▲▼	▲▼	▲▼	▲▼	▲▼	▲▼	▲▼

Think about your week.
Circle the up triangle if you improved even a little this past week.

For example: Did you spend even a little more time doing any type of exercise this week?

In this chapter, I hope to make a compelling case for you to up your exercise game. I hope I can convince you that exercise is the number one treatment/intervention for prevention of most physical and psychological problems. I will lay out six reasons to get your exercise going and share exercise guidelines from the National Institutes of Health (NIH), Centers for Disease Control and Prevention (CDC), and the American Heart Association (AHA). In addition, you will find some amazing conclusions from several large national and international studies. I provide summaries from what I consider to be two of the most important recent books reviewing the latest science on exercise: *Spark* by John Ratey, MD, and *Spring Chicken* by Bill Gifford, as well as an overview of the "Exercise as Medicine" website by the American College of Sports Medicine (ACSM).

Six Reasons to Exercise: Which Ones are Most Important to You?

- Lower inflammatory levels
- Stronger immune system
- Helps maintain telomeres
- Improves your cell's ability to clean up waste and reduce free radicals
- Raises levels of brain-derived neurotrophic factor (BDNF) and other brain growth factors
- Charges up your mitochondria (the energy producing part of each cell)

Each of these six benefits alone should be enough to motivate us to exercise more, but taken together, they provide a very compelling call to action.

The Looking Good/Feeling Good (LGFG) tool is built around the notion that the top five items—nutrition, fun/play, exercise, social support, and rest/sleep—all impact your energy and mood. Exercise may have the most dramatic impact on your energy in part because it has a direct effect on your mitochondria. Let's take a look at these energy factories found inside our cells.

Stay Fit, Stay Young, Stay Energized: The Role of Exercise and Mitochondria

Exercise evokes a multisystem response that leads to health outcomes and can reverse the deleterious effects of disuse and aging. It is currently widely accepted that exercise is medicine.

Exercise is a physical activity that works the body at greater intensity than usual movements. To work at higher intensity, the body, particularly the skeletal muscles and the cardiovascular system, requires an extra supply of energy. Mitochondria are the main energy suppliers that coordinate cellular processes for sustaining body activity during exercise. Therefore, exercise and mitochondria are in a close relationship and influence each other. The more you exercise, the more energy you have.

Mitochondria and ATP

Exercise causes mitochondria to generate more ATP for contracting muscles, and thus, increases our available energy. *Adenosine triphosphate* (ATP) is a nucleotide used in cells as a coenzyme. It is often called the "molecular unit of currency." ATP transports chemical energy within cells for metabolism. Every cell uses ATP for energy.

Mitochondria generate ATP by utilizing the energy released during the oxidation of the food we eat. ATP is used in turn as the primary energy source for most biochemical and physiological processes, such as growth, movement, and homeostasis. For more information, visit: www.ncbi.nlm.nih.gov

The Role of Mitochondrial Function and Cellular Bioenergetics

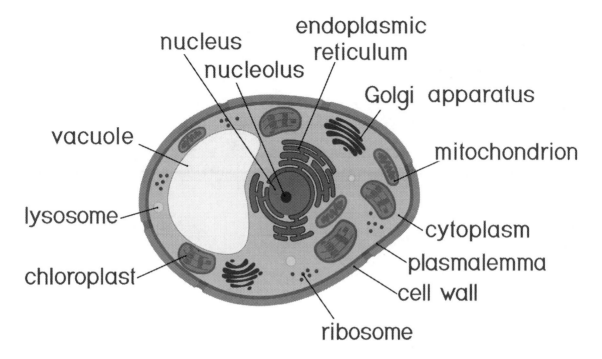

Mitochondria are often referred to as the powerhouses of the cell. They help turn the energy we take from food into energy that the cell can use. Below are some quick facts:

- Average number of mitochondria per cell = 200
- Up to 10,000 in some specialized cells

For a useful resource on mitochondria, read Tim Newman's (2018) article in *MedicalNewsToday*: https://www.medicalnewstoday.com/articles/320875.php

Rev up your energy

Mitochondria are running the show so take good care of your mitochondria. Without healthy mitochondria, we have little or no energy. Exercise and a healthy diet are two of our best ways to ensure our mitochondria are healthy and happy. The main role of eating is to provide the fuel for mitochondria, and the main role of breathing is to provide the oxygen and to remove the carbon dioxide produced by mitochondria. Similarly, a major role of the cardiovascular system is to deliver key ingredients (glucose, fatty acids, and oxygen) and remove the products (carbon dioxide) of mitochondrial activity. Be kind to your mitochondria by exercising daily, and you will feel a surge in your energy level.

Exercise, Your Cardio Health, and Maximum Oxygen Uptake (VO2 Max)

VO2 max, also known as maximal oxygen uptake, is the measurement of the *maximum* amount of oxygen a person can utilize during intense exercise. It is a common measurement used to establish the aerobic endurance of an athlete prior to or during the course of training. VO2 max is generally regarded as the best indicator of cardiorespiratory fitness. The higher your VO2 max, the more oxygen your body can use—and the better your aerobic fitness.

Turn Back Time!

A person's VO2 max typically declines with age. Usually the peak is around your 20s, and sometime in your 30s, VO2 max starts to decline, approximately by 10 percent per decade. However, it is possible to boost your VO2 max and turn back the clock. The recipe is simple: aerobic exercise improves VO2 max, whereas a sedentary lifestyle leads to low cardiorespiratory fitness. If your VO2 max is below average for your age group, your fitness age is older than your actual age and vice versa. If you have a good capacity for aerobic endurance, you might be much younger than your driver's license says.

"If we had a pill that contained all of the benefits of exercise, it would be the most widely prescribed drug in the world."

—Ronald M. Davis, MD, American Medical Association Past President

According to Herman Bonner (2020), Communications Specialist of *Firstbeat*:

> You won't find many people willing to argue that physical activity is bad for you. That said, a healthy, sustainable approach means getting the dosage right. Results matter. In terms of understanding whether your activity and lifestyle profile translates into real health benefits, VO2max – the defining metric of cardiorespiratory fitness (CRF) – is a perfect resource. How important is your fitness level? It's so important that in 2016 the American Heart Association published an official scientific statement recommending that clinicians routinely measure VO2max and consider it as a vital sign, along with traditional measures like body temperature, blood pressure, and heart and respiration rates.

Getting older is a fact of life, but regular exercise and an active lifestyle can immunize you from many of the effects of aging. It's no accident that the same types of activities that boost your fitness level also minimize muscle loss, keep your bones strong, and even keep your brain healthy. Multiple studies have also linked higher VO2 max scores with reduced risk of developing both dementia and Alzheimer's disease (Bonner, 2020). Research also shows that it's never too late to benefit from regular exercise, even for those who haven't been active in the past.

Your fitness level has a significant impact on your susceptibility to disease and overall health. People with higher fitness levels experience lower rates of cardiovascular and coronary artery disease, colon cancer, and type-2 diabetes. Bonner (2020) asserts that those findings from the AHA are supported by additional research which revealed that a "10% increase in VO2max could decrease all-cause mortality risk by 15%."

Exercise is a well-known method of stress management, but a higher fitness level can even prevent physiological stress from accumulating in the first place. People who are more physically active experience less physiological stress and are more resilient to the impacts of stress when it does arise. There is a clear link between regular physical activity and feelings of personal well-being.

> "Most Americans don't burn out, they rust from inactivity. The
> human body desperately needs activity and exercise: and the exercise
> that is most vital to our well-being is aerobic exercise."
> —Ken Matheny and Richard Riordan, *Stress and Strategies for Lifestyle Management*

Spark: The Revolutionary New Science of Exercise and the Brain

Spark: The Revolutionary New Science of Exercise and the Brain is my favorite resource for the new science around exercise. John Ratey, MD, a Harvard psychiatrist, does an excellent job of summarizing the science of how exercise cues the building blocks of learning in the brain and how it affects mood, anxiety, and attention. In addition, he explains how exercise guards against stress and reverses some of the effects of aging. Ratey (2013) asserts, "the point of exercise is to condition the brain" (p. 3).

Exercise increases levels of important neurotransmitters: serotonin, norepinephrine, and dopamine. These are crucial for thinking and emotions. Lack of serotonin is associated with depression. Ratey (2013) cites a Duke University (2000) study that found exercise to be better than Zoloft for treating depression: "Exercise has a profound effect on cognitive ability and mental health. It is the best treatment we have for most psychiatric problems" (p. 7).

Exercise unleashes a cascade of neurochemicals and growth factors and bolsters the brain's infrastructure. The brain responds like a muscle. It grows with use and withers with inactivity. The neurons in the brain connect to one another through "leaves" on tree-like branches. Exercise causes these branches to grow and bloom new buds, which enhances brain functioning at the cellular level. Your brain runs the show of your body and mind—so improving its functioning is of monumental importance.

I want to walk you through a little brain chemistry-related exercise that I think you will find fascinating. Looking at the impact of exercise from inside brain cells, exercise produces proteins that travel through the bloodstream and into the brain, where they play pivotal roles in the mechanisms of higher thought processes. Some of these proteins and hormones include *brain-derived neurotrophic factor* (BDNF), *insulin growth factor* (IGF-1), and *vascular endothelial growth factor* (VEGF).

Brain-derived neurotrophic factor (BDNF)

- BDNF is a protein produced inside nerve cells when they are active.
- It keeps neurons functioning and growing and spurs growth of new neurons.
- Exercise increases BDNF levels.
- BDNF is a brain growth factor:
  o Like fertilizer for your brain's neurons
  o One of a class of master molecules in a family of proteins called factors (BDNF is the most prominent)
  o While neurotransmitters carry out signaling, neurotrophins, such as BDNF, build and maintain the cell circuitry (the brain infrastructure)

Grow your dendrites with exercise. Dendrites are like branches of a tree, extending from the body of the neuron and opening into gradually smaller projections. At the end of these projections are the synapses, where the information transfer between neurons occurs. The following includes benefits and characteristics of BDNF:

- BDNF improves memory by increasing dendrite branches.
- BDNF promotes brain growth and development.
- BDNF drives brain plasticity and neuron survival.
- BDNF acts in the hippocampus and may improve neurodegenerative diseases, such as Huntington's disease, Alzheimer's disease, bipolar disorder, and depression.

- Chronic stress depletes BDNF.
- Exercise increases BDNF.

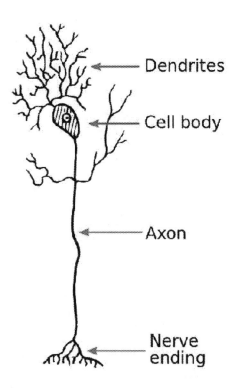

Exercise and Human Growth Factor (HGH)

Human growth factor (HGH) is a hormone considered vital to the growth and development of all cells in the brain and the body. Below are some unique traits:

- HGH counteracts the natural cellular atrophy of aging.
- HGH is what life-extension groups call "the fountain of youth."
- HGH decreases as we age
- Exercise counters this decrease by increasing production of HGH

Plasticity of brain is an important concept. The brain is flexible and can actually be molded by inputs we provide. It is like a muscle that can be sculpted. The more you use it, the stronger and more flexible it gets. Exercise optimizes plasticity.

Ratey (2013) teaches us how to be our own brain electrician. Aerobic exercise increases BDNF, reverses memory decline in the elderly, and actually increases the growth of new brain cells in the brain's memory center. Aerobic exercise turns on genes linked to longevity and targets the gene that codes for BDNF, the brain growth hormone. Exercise builds a brain that resists physical shrinkage and enhances cognitive flexibility. Here are five key benefits of exercise for the brain: helps control inflammation, increases insulin sensitivity, influences better blood sugar control, expands the size of the memory center, and boosts BDNF levels. Exercisers have reduced levels of C-reactive protein (a common marker of inflammation).

Our thoughts, behavior, and environment influence the pattern of connection of our neurons and re-wire these neuron connections constantly, and exercise is critically important to our brain's health. So, we have seen how exercise impacts the structure and function of our brains and influences how we feel and how much energy we have. But how much exercise is needed for optimal health?

National Institutes of Health ([NIH], 2015–2020) Guidelines for Exercise

- 30 minutes of moderate to vigorous activity 5 or more days per week
- Examples of various exercises that can meet these guidelines include: walking, dancing, biking, skating, yoga, jogging, strength training, swimming, and tennis

Center for Disease Control ([CDC], 2020) and American Heart Association ([AHA], 2018) Guidelines for Exercise

The CDC (2020) and AHA (2018) recommendations for exercise are close to the NIH's (2015–2020) guidelines:

- 150 minutes of moderate aerobic exercise; or
- 75 minutes of vigorous exercise; and
- Strength building exercise at least twice per week

Notice that the CDC's (2020) and AHA's (2018) recommendations includes "75 minutes of vigorous exercise," which equals 150 minutes of moderate exercise, and that they include strength training, which is not listed by NIH (2015–2020) guidelines.

In case you are thinking of leaving off strength training, consider that the following is what we know about the many benefits strength training:

- Maintains bone density
- Keeps body fat low
- Reduces anxiety and depression
- Improves cognitive function
- Lowers risk of cardiovascular disease and cancer

"Exercise: The Miracle Cure," Academy of Medical Royal Colleges (2015) Made Headlines

According to the Academy of Medical Royal Colleges (2015), there is "overwhelming evidence" that "30 minutes of moderate exercise five times per week improves health and prevents many common diseases, reducing the risk of each of them between 20–50%" and also "reduces risk of dementia, stroke, and osteoporosis by 30% each" (p. 39). I think one can make the case that exercise is our #1 intervention for a long and healthy life. Here is some additional information about the right dose of exercise and how exercise affects brain functioning.

The Right Dose of Exercise

The Goldilocks problem about exercise: not too little, not too much, try to get it just right to improve health and longevity. The current guidelines from U.S. government and health organizations suggest 150 minutes of moderate exercise per week to build and maintain health and fitness. This is roughly 30 minutes a day, five days a week, or a little more than 20 minutes per day, seven days per week. Two recent large studies shed some light on whether or not this dosage should be our best target. Published in *The Journal of American Medical Association (JAMA) Internal Medicine* in 2015, researchers at the National Cancer Institute at Harvard University, along with other institutions, collaborated in sharing data about people's exercise habits derived from six large, ongoing health surveys. Arem et al. (2015) included over 600,000 adults, most of whom were middle age. This group was divided into subgroups, all the way from those not exercising at all to those exercising 25 hours per week or more.

Arem et al. (2015) looked at 14 years' worth of death records for the group. To no one's surprise, they found that the non-exercisers were at the greatest risk of death. Those exercising a little (but less than the recommended 150 hours per week) lowered their risk of dying during the 14 years by 20%. Those who met the 150 minutes per week guidelines had a reduced death risk of 31% (compared to the non-exercising group). The Goldilocks (just right, sweet spot) amount of exercise seemed to be those who tripled the recommended 150 minutes per week by exercising moderately (mostly by walking) for 450 minutes per week (a little more than one hour per day). This group were 39% less likely to die during this 14-year span than the non-exercise group. Exercising beyond the 450 minutes per week generally did not provide additional death risk reduction (Arem et al., 2015).

> "As time goes on, paper after paper after paper shows that the most effective,
> potent way we can improve quality of life and duration of life is exercise."
> —Mark Tarnopolsky, a genetic neurologist at McMaster University, Ontario, Canada
> (as cited in Oaklander, 2016)

Mark Tarnopolsky is convinced that the benefits of exercise (such as slower aging, better mood, less chronic pain, stronger vision, and others) are real, measurable, and almost immediate.

Here are some findings from a second large study of 200,000 Australian adults also looking at the amount of exercise and its correlation to the risk of dying, which found similar results. Gebel et al. (2015), researchers at the James Cook University in Cairns, found that those meeting the 150 minute per week guidelines substantially reduced their risk of death.

This Australian study found that rigorous exercise also gained a small but important additional reduction in mortality. Those spending 30% of their weekly exercise time in activities such as running, playing, or engaging in competitive singles tennis, versus walking, were 9% less likely to die prematurely than those doing only moderate exercising for the same amount of time (Gebel et al., 2015). Those spending more than 30% of their exercise time in vigorous exercise gained an extra 13% reduction compared with those who only exercised moderately. It appears that anyone capable of exercising 150 minutes per week, who can include 20–30 minutes of vigorous activity, gain significant protection against premature death (Gebel et al., 2015).

A third study with 70,000 patients of the Henry Ford Hospital in Detroit found that poor cardiovascular fitness, combined with other risk factors, increases the risk of death by over 33% (Shaya et al., 2016). The Henry Ford Exercise Testing Project (FIT) was the largest study of cardiorespiratory fitness to date. Shaya et al. (2016) looked at patients ages 18–96 who underwent treadmill stress test between 1991–2009. They used 58,818 patients who had no history of coronary blockages or heart failure. They compared patient's cardiorespiratory fitness level to their risk factors for cardiovascular disease: age, sex, HDL, cholesterol levels, race, systolic blood pressure, smoking, blood pressure medication, substance use, and diabetes. Those with highest cardio-risk factor scores and lowest fitness levels were 34% more likely to die prematurely than those with the lowest risk factor scores and highest fitness level scores. They also found that good cardiorespiratory fitness is associated with lower death rates, regardless of a person's risk factor scores.

Exercise and Brain Functioning

A University of Kansas (KU) Medical Center randomized study of adults age 65 and over, led by James Burns, MD, co-director of KU Alzheimer's Disease Center, found improved brain functioning with increased fitness levels (Vidoni et al., 2015). This six-month long study with healthy adults, who showed no cognitive decline, investigated what is the ideal amount of exercise required to have significant benefits for brain health. Vidoni et al. (2015) divided the adults into four groups: one control that did not monitor exercise, one that moderately exercised for the recommended 150 minutes per week, one that exercised for 75 minutes per week, and one that exercised for 225 minutes per week. They found that all three exercising groups saw benefits, with those exercising more gaining more benefits involving attention levels, ability to focus, and visual-spatial processing. For brain functioning, the takeaway seems to be similar to the risk of death finding, which is the more exercise you do, the more benefit gained for your brain. Any aerobic exercise was good and more was better. They also found that intensity of exercise is more important than duration. It is not enough to exercise more. You must exercise in a way that bumps up your fitness level.

Spring Chicken: Stay Young Forever or Die Trying

In the book, *Spring Chicken: Stay Young Forever or Die Trying*, Bill Gifford writes entertainingly about the how we all can keep ourselves healthy and vibrant as we age. I wanted to specifically share with you some of the gems I picked up from him on exercise.

Here is one of my happiest discoveries: **Dedicated exercisers can retain into their sixties and seventies up to 80% of the capacity they had in their prime, whereas the sedentary retain only around 22% of physical capacity.** Exercising is more about staying healthy than winning races. The more intensity of the exercise, the slower you will lose your physical ability. Exercise is one of the secrets to longevity. Exercise is anti-inflammatory.

Since fast twitch muscles decline more quickly than slow twitch, shoot for a combined exercise program that includes endurance as well as coordination (tennis, ping pong, b-ball, juggling, and dancing). The fitter you are, the longer you get to actively participate in life. Sitting is the new smoking—a bad habit that leads to disease.

Gifford (2016) highlights Melov et al. (2007), a Canadian study that found that exercise actually reversed the effects of aging in older Canadians. The sample was divided into two groups—one older and one younger. Muscle biopsies were taken, and gene expression patterns in tissues were analyzed to determine which genes were turned on and off. Then, half of the members in each group were placed on a strict, but not too demanding, resistance exercise program. After six months, more biopsies found the older subjects' muscles had reverted to a younger state—that is, they had many of the same genes activated as their younger study mates. **The conclusion: You can reverse gene expression of aging with exercise. In short, exercise had switched the young genes on and the old genes off.** Most of the genes had to do with the function of mitochondria—the little energy plants inside our cells.

A follow-up study by Mark Tarnopolsky, one of Melov et al.'s (2007) coauthors, at Ontario's McMaster University, looked specifically at mitochondria in mice (Kolesar et al., 2014). This study also found that exercise reversed aging by repairing mitochondria DNA. *Mitochondrial dysfunction* is believed to be one of the primary drivers of aging. As we lose mitochondria with age, we run out of energy.

One would think that this kind of evidence would motivate most to "up" their exercise. Unfortunately, 90% of Americans fail to meet the minimal guidelines for physical activity, defined by the federal government as 30 minutes of moderate exercise (i.e. brisk walking), 5 times per week. Even a little bit helps. Exercise is our best medicine to fight aging.

Exercise is now considered a medical intervention. The LIFE Study (Pahor et al., 2014) involved 800 sedentary older people age 70–89 who began mild exercise. They were already in trouble, scoring very low on physical performance tests, but they could at least walk a quarter mile. They were close to being unable to live independently. After two years, the exercise group had far lower rates of disability than the matched group who had been simply told to exercise. A little bit of walking had kept many of them out of the nursing home. Gifford (2016) concludes that exercise is our most promising intervention for the ills of aging—and it's free!

Another good source of current scientific information about exercise can be found at the Exercise is Medicine® (EIM) website: www.exerciseismedicine.org

EIM is a global health initiative managed by the American College of Sports Medicine (ACSM). Its goal is to make physical activity assessment and promotion a standard in clinical care, connecting health care with evidence-based physical activity resources for people everywhere and of all abilities. EIM encourages physicians and other health care providers to include physical activity when designing treatment plans and to refer patients to evidence-based exercise programs and qualified exercise professionals. EIM is committed to the belief that physical activity promotes optimal health and is integral in the prevention and treatment of many medical conditions.

References

Academy of Medical Royal Colleges. (2015). *Exercise: The miracle cure and the role of the doctor in promoting it.* https://www.aomrc.org.uk/wp-content/uploads/2016/ 05/Exercise_the_ Miracle_Cure_0215. pdf

American Heart Association. (2018). *How much physical activity do you need?* https://www.heart. org/en/healthy-living/fitness/fitness-basics/aha-recs-for-physical-activity-infographic

Arem, H., Moore, S. C., Patel, A., Hartge, P., Berrington de Gonzalez, A., Visvanathan, K., Campbell, P., Freedman, M., Weiderpass, E., Olov Adami, H., Linet, M., Lee, M., & Matthews, C. (2015). Leisure time physical activity and mortality: A detailed pooled analysis of the dose-response relationship. *JAMA Intern Med., 175*(6), 959–967. http:// doi:10.1001/jamainternmed.2015.0533

Bonner, H. (2020). *5 reasons to boost your VO2 max*. Firstbeat. https://www.firstbeat.com/en/blog/5-reasons-boost-vo2max/

Brand, M. D., Orr, A. L., Perevoshchikova, I. V., & Quinlan, C. L. (2013). The role of mitochondrial function and cellular bioenergetics in ageing and disease. *The British Journal of Dermatology, 169*(2), 1–8. https://doi.org/10.1111/bjd.12208 Brigman, G., Villares, E., & Webb, L. (2018). *Looking good/feeling good* [Infographic].

Evidence-based school counseling: A student success approach. Routledge.

Center for Disease Control. (2020). *Physical activity*. https://www.cdc.gov/physicalactivity/basics/index.htm

Exercise is Medicine. (2020). *Exercise is Medicine: American College of Sports Medicine*. www.exerciseismedicine.org

Gebel, K., Ding, D., Chey, T., Stamatakis, E., Brown, W., & Bauman, A. (2015). Effect of moderate to vigorous physical activity on all-cause mortality in middle-aged and older Australians. *JAMA Intern. Med., 175*(6), 970–977. http://doi:10.1001/jamainternmed.2015.0541

Gifford, B. (2016). *Spring chicken: Stay young forever (or die trying)*. Grand Central Publishing.

Kolesar, J. E., Safdar, A., Abadi, A., MacNeil, L. G., Crane, J. D., Tarnopolsky, M. A., & Kaufman, B. A. (2014). Defects in mitochondrial DNA replication and oxidative damage in muscle of mtDNA mutator mice. *Free Radical Biology & Medicine, 75*, 241–51. http://doi: 10.1016/ j.freeradbiomed.2014.07.038

Matheny, K., & Riordan, R. (1992). *Stress and strategies for lifestyle management*. Georgia State University Press.

Melov, S., Tarnopolsky, M., Beckman, K., Felkey, K., & Hubbard, A. (2007). Resistance exercise reverses aging in human skeletal muscle. *PLoS ONE, 2*(5), e465. http://doi: 10.1371/journal.pone.0000465

National Institutes of Health. (2015–2020). *Dietary guidelines 2015–2020*. https://health.gov/our-work/food-nutrition/2015-2020-dietary-guidelines/guidelines/appendix-1/

Newman, T. (2018, February 8). What are mitochondria? *MedicalNewsToday*. https://www.medicalnewstoday.com/articles/320875

Oaklander, M. (2016). The new science of exercise. *Time*. https://time.com/4475628/the-new- science-of-exercise/

Pahor, M., Guralnik, J. M., Ambrosius, W. T., Blair, S., Bonds, D. E., Church, T. S., Espeland, M. A., Fielding, R. A., Gill, T. M., Groessl, E. J., Kritchevsky, S. B., Manini, T. M., McDermott, M. M., Miller, M. E., Newman, A. B., Rejeski, W. J., Sink, K. M., & Williamson, J. D. (2014). Effect of structured physical activity on prevention of major mobility disability in older adults: The LIFE study randomized clinical trial. *JAMA*, *311*(23), 2387–96. http://doi: 10.1001/jama.2014.5616

Ratey, J. (2013). *Spark: The revolutionary new science of exercise and the brain.* Little, Brown and Company.

Shaya, G., Al-Mallah, M., Hung, R., Khurram, N., Blumenthal, R., Ehrman, J., Keteyian, S., Brawner, C., Qureshi, W., & Blaha, M. (2016). High exercise capacity attenuates the risk of early mortality after a first myocardial infarction. *Mayo Clinic Proceedings*, *91*(2), 129–139.

U.S. Department of Health and Human Services. (2008). *Physical activity guidelines for Americans.* https://health.gov/our-work/physical-activity.

Vidoni, E., Johnson, D., Morris, J., Van Sciver, A., Greer, C., Billinger, S., Donnelly, J., & Burns, Jeffrey. (2015). Dose-response of aerobic exercise on cognition: A community-based, pilot randomized controlled trial. *PLoS ONE*, *10*(7): 1–13. http://doi:10.1371/ journal. pone.0131647

CHAPTER 4

SOCIAL SUPPORT

"The most important gifts you can give are your love, time and attention. Slow down, take time to smile and enjoy loved ones…life goes by way too fast."
—Nishan Panwar (as cited by Robin, n.d.)

Chapter Highlights:

- Three Famous Psychologists - Importance of Belonging, Art of Loving, and Keys to Happy Marriage
- Good Genes Are Nice, but Joy Is Better: Takeaways From the Harvard Longitudinal Study
- "Social Relations & Health: A Flashpoint for Health Policy"
- Three Important Ways Social Relationships Benefit Health: Behavioral, Psychological, and Physiological
- APA Psychology Help Center
- "My Social Support Network"
- The Lubben Social Network Scale

Could social support be one of the most important factors in your overall health and happiness? Several authoritative sources point strongly in that direction. Social support has been defined in a number of ways. Here are some key domains within the category of social support: emotional support, affirmation, assistance, intimacy, comfort, and physical affection.

Famous psychologist Alfred Adler built his theory around the notion that we are social beings and that belonging is a primary need. According to Adler (1964), we all want to belong and be significant. Belonging to groups reduces a sense of isolation and loneliness that can be a part of the human condition. We are programed to live in social groups because historically we needed the group to survive. Adler used the term *social interest* to explain the need to contribute and give back to the group and move beyond our own self-interest. While social interest has altruistic elements, a sense of psychological well-being accrues from transcending self-centered preoccupations. Finding meaning and purpose in life by participating in endeavors beyond oneself is a key aspect of social interest

In 1956, another famous psychologist, Erik Fromm, wrote a landmark book, *The Art of Loving*. I recently came upon a blog by John Messerly, PhD, who writes on the topic of love, and shared this from a quote from Fromm:

> Is love an art? Then it requires knowledge and effort. Or is love a pleasant sensation, which to experience is a matter of chance, something one "falls into" if one is lucky? This little book is based on the former premise, while undoubtedly the majority of people today believe it is the latter. (as cited in Messerly, 2014)

According to Messerly (2014), Fromm thought that we often misunderstand love for a variety of reasons. First, we see the problem of love as one of being loved rather than one of loving. We try to be richer, more popular, or more attractive instead of learning how to love. Second, we think of love in terms of finding an object to love, rather than of it being a faculty to cultivate. We think it is hard to find someone to love, but easy to love, when in fact the opposite is true. (Think of movies where after a long search the lovers finally connect and then the movie ends. But it's the happily ever after that's the hard part). Finally, we don't distinguish between "falling" in love and what Fromm calls "standing" in love. If two previously isolated people suddenly discover each other, it is exhilarating—but such feelings don't last. Real love involves standing in love; it is an art we learn after years of practice, just as we would learn any other art or skill. *Real love is not something we fall into, it is something we learn how to do.* In the end, though loving is difficult to learn and practice, it is most worthwhile and more important than money, fame, or power. For the mystery of existence reveals itself, if it ever does, through our relationships with nature, productive work and, most of all, through our relationships with other people. Thus, to experience the depths of life, we should cultivate the art of loving.

More recently, John Gottman, PhD, has been one of most prolific researchers on what makes relationships work. His 35 years of research on couples and relationships provides some concrete guidelines to help us stay on track for healthy and sustainable relationships. Here are two key findings of Gottman's 35 years of research:

1. Happily married couples behave like good friends, and they handle their conflicts in gentle, positive ways.
2. Happily married couples are able to repair negative interactions during an argument, and they are able to process negative emotions fully.

Gottman, now a Professor Emeritus at the University of Washington, has studied more than 3,000 couples in research (including divorce prediction research) and 4,000 more couples in intervention and treatment research. In addition, he and his wife, Julie Gottman, PhD, have worked with approximately 8,000 couples in workshop and therapy settings. Fourteen-thousand clinicians worldwide have been trained in the Gottman Method. He was recently voted one of the "Top 10 Most Influential Therapists" of the past quarter-century by the publication, *Psychotherapy Networker.*

I highly recommend three of his many books: New York Times bestseller, *The Seven Principles for Making Marriage Work* (Crown Publishers); *The Relationship Cure, A 5-Step Guide for Building Better Connections with Family, Friends, and Lovers* (Crown Publishers); and *What Predicts Divorce* (Psychology Press). Within *The Seven Principles for Making Marriage Work*, Gottman and Silver (1999) discusses the negative behaviors that predict divorce, which he calls "The Four Horsemen of the Apocalypse":

*   Criticism: Stating your complaints as a defect in your partner's personality, i.e. "You always talk about yourself. You are so selfish" (Gottman & Silver, 1999, p. 32).

- Contempt: Statements that come from a relative position of superiority. Contempt is the greatest predictor of divorce and should be eliminated if you want the relationship to survive. Examples: "You are an idiot," you say, rolling your eyes after your partner speaks (Gottman & Silver, 1999, p. 34).
- Defensiveness: Self-protection in the form of righteous indignation or innocent victimhood. Defensiveness wards off a perceived attack. Example: "It's not my fault that we're always late, it's your fault" (Gottman & Silver, 1999, p. 36).
- Stonewalling: Emotional withdrawal from interaction. Example: The listener does not give the speaker the usual non-verbal signals that the listener is "tracking" the speaker.

Gottman also recommends a ratio of five to one positive comments/actions for every negative comment/action. This is needed to repair the break in the relationship caused by the negative comment/action (Gottman & Silver, 1999, p. 38).

So, if the above four are the most important habits to avoid broken relations and divorce, what advice does Gottman's research reveal for healthy and successful marriage? The quote and seven principles below are from Gottman and Silver (1999):

> It soon became apparent that these happy marriages were never perfect unions. Some couples who said they were very satisfied with each other still had significant differences in temperament, interests, and family values. Conflict was not infrequent. They argued, just as the unhappy couple did, over money, jobs, kids, housekeeping, sex, and in-laws. The mystery was how they so adroitly navigated their way through these difficulties and kept their marriages happy and stable.

> It took studying hundreds of couples to uncover the secrets of these emotionally intelligent marriages. No two marriages are the same, but the more closely my research team and I looked at happy marriages, the more evident it became that they were alike in seven telltale ways. Happily married couples may not be aware that they follow these Seven Principles, but they all do. Unhappy marriages always came up short in at least one of these seven areas—and usually in many of them. By mastering these Seven Principles, you can ensure that your own marriage will thrive. (in section, "What Does Make Marriage Work?")

Note: Gottman and Silver (1999) has a chapter devoted to each of these seven principles:

Principle 1: Enhance Your Love Maps. How well do you know your partner? Thriving couples have a thorough "Love Map" of their partner's dreams, values, and essence. (p. 52).

Principle 2: Nurture Your Fondness and Admiration. How much do you really like your partner? Thriving couples nurture a deep sense of fondness and admiration. They cherish one another. One way to do this is find out from your partner 7 things you do or can do that would show you care, love, adore, respect, appreciate and think they are important. (p. 67)

Principle 3: Turn Toward Each Other Instead of Away. Happy couples consistently find ways to CONNECT—they are attuning themselves to one another by *turning toward* each other. (p. 87)

Principle 4: Let Your Partner Influence You. Happy couples embody a willingness to yield in order to win—they let one another influence each other and don't always need to be domineeringly "right." (p. 115)

Principle 5: Solve Your Solvable Problems. There are two types of problems: solvable and perpetual. (Surprisingly, 69% are unsolvable!) And... There are some key practices to resolving the solvable ones! (p. 160).

Principle 6: Overcome Gridlock. Then there are the unsolvable problems—the perpetual ones. We need to work to overcome gridlock so these differences (that exist in ALL relationships and form the bulk of what we argue about) don't become *irreconcilable* differences. (p. 237).

Principle 7: Create Shared Meaning. Happy couples embrace the four pillars of shared meaning: rituals of connection + support for each other's roles + shared goals + shared values and symbols. (p. 260).

I highly recommend *Seven Principles for Making Marriage Work*. I have used it and given it to many of my friends and family.

Friendship is another major source of our social support system. We define friendship as "connections with others in a non-sexual manner and being able to give and receive emotional support." Gottman and DeClaire (2001) also offers these five tips building our friendship network and helping us connect with others in his excellent book, *The Relationship Cure, A 5-Step Guide for Building Better Connections with Family, Friends, and Lovers*:

- Exercise buddies: This is a twofer. You get social time and the benefit of a healthy habit.
- Standing date: The bestselling *Tuesdays with Morrie* helps illuminate the power of regularly meeting with your friend no matter what. If not weekly, perhaps bi-weekly, or monthly.
- Volunteer together: Another twofer that nurtures a friendship and contributes to the community. Whether it's a foodbank, voting poll on election day, or serving on a committee at church, this is win-win strategy.
- Support groups/book clubs: Find an interest you share with one or more friends and meet regularly to pursue it.
- Spiritual practice: Still another twofer that nurtures friendships while connecting to something larger than ourselves.

Which of these five friendship network tips do you already use, and which ones look promising enough to give a try?

Good Genes Are Nice, But Joy Is Better: Takeaways From the Harvard Longitudinal Study Highlighting the Importance of Relationships

What if there was a study dedicated to unearthing the secrets to a happy and purposeful life? It would have to be conducted over the course of many decades, following the lives of real people from childhood until old age, in order to see how they changed and what they learned about some of life's fundamental questions: how we grow and change, what we value as time goes on, and what is likely to make us happy and fulfilled. The following is a summary of just one such kind of a study, which appeared in the Harvard Gazette in 2017: "Good Genes are Nice, but Joy is Better: Takeaways from the Harvard Longitudinal Study Highlighting the Importance of Relationships."

Over 80 years ago, scientists began tracking the health of 268 Harvard sophomores, hoping the longitudinal study would reveal clues to leading healthy and happy lives. The study included only men to begin with, since Harvard was all male at the time. The Harvard Study of Adult Development, one of the longest studies of adult life ever done, has amassed a treasure trove of data on physical and mental health, and includes the Grant and Glueck studies. The Harvard Study has expanded to include the participants' offspring, who now number 1,300 and are in their 50s and 60s. Some participants went on to become successful businessmen, doctors, lawyers, and others ended up as schizophrenics or alcoholics, but not on inevitable tracks. According to Mineo (2017):

> Over several decades, the control groups have expanded. During the 1970s, 456 inner-city residents of Boston were enlisted as part of the Glueck Study, and more than a decade ago, researchers began including wives in the Grant and Glueck studies.

> "The surprising finding is that our relationships and how happy we are in our relationships has a powerful influence on our health," said Robert Waldinger, one of the directors of the study, a psychiatrist at Massachusetts General Hospital and a professor of psychiatry at Harvard Medical School. "Taking care of your body is important, but tending to your relationships is a form of self-care too. That, I think, is the revelation."

> Close relationships, more than money or fame, are what keep people happy throughout their lives, the study revealed. Those ties protect people from life's discontents, help to delay mental and physical decline, and are better predictors of long and happy lives than social class, IQ, or even genes. That finding proved true across the board among both the Harvard men and the inner-city participants.

The longitudinal study research has been largely financed by grants from the National Institutes of Health, first through the National Institute of Mental Health (NIMH), and more recently through the National Institute on Aging (NIA). In the words of Mineo (2017):

Researchers who have pored through data set, including vast medical records and hundreds of in-person interviews and questionnaires, found a strong correlation between men's flourishing lives and their relationships with family, friends, and community. Several studies found that people's level of satisfaction with their relationships at age 50 was a better predictor of physical health than their cholesterol levels were.

"When we gathered together everything we knew about them about at age 50, it wasn't their middle-age cholesterol levels that predicted how they were going to grow old," said Waldinger in a popular TED Talk. "It was how satisfied they were in their relationships. The people who were the most satisfied in their relationships at age 50 were the healthiest at age 80."

So, the quality of our social support systems have a direct and strong impact on our overall physical and mental health. I highly recommend Waldinger's (2015) TED Talk, "What Makes a Good Life? Lessons from the Longest Study on Happiness." It has been viewed over 13,000,000 times.

The Harvard researchers found that marital satisfaction has a protective effect on people's mental health. They found that people who had happy marriages in their 80s reported that their moods didn't suffer even on the days when they had more physical pain. As explained by Mineo (2017):

Those who had unhappy marriages felt both more emotional and physical pain. Those who kept warm relationships got to live longer and happier, said Waldinger, and the loners often died earlier. "Loneliness kills," he said. "It's as powerful as smoking or alcoholism." (Mineo, 2017, p. 82)

"Aging is a continuous process," Waldinger said. "You can see how people can start to differ in their health trajectory in their 30s, so that by taking good care of yourself early in life you can set yourself on a better course for aging. The best advice I can give is 'Take care of your body as though you were going to need it for 100 years,' because you might."

The study has had four directors. Mineo (2017) elaborates:

Under the first director, Clark Heath, who stayed from 1938 until 1954, the study mirrored the era's dominant view of genetics and biological determinism. Early researchers believed that physical constitution, intellectual ability, and personality traits determined adult development. They made detailed anthropometric measurements of skulls, brow bridges, and moles, wrote in-depth notes on the functioning of major organs, examined brain activity through electroencephalograms, and even analyzed the men's handwriting.

Now, researchers draw men's blood for DNA testing and put them into MRI scanners to examine organs and tissues in their bodies, procedures that would have sounded like science fiction back in 1938. In that sense, the study itself represents a history of the changes that life brings.

Psychiatrist George Vaillant, who joined the team as a researcher in 1966, led the study from 1972 until 2004. Trained as a psychoanalyst, Vaillant emphasized the role of relationships, and came to recognize the crucial role they played in people living long and pleasant lives.

"When the study began, nobody cared about empathy or attachment. But the key to healthy aging is relationships, relationships, relationships."— George Vaillant

In a 2002 book called "Aging Well," Vaillant wrote that six factors predicted healthy aging for the Harvard men: physical activity, absence of alcohol abuse and smoking, having mature mechanisms to cope with life's ups and downs, and enjoying both a healthy weight and a stable marriage. For the inner-city men, education was an additional factor.

"The more education an Inner City man obtained," wrote Vaillant, "the more likely they he was to stop smoking, eat sensibly, and be circumspect in his use of alcohol" (Valliant, 2012, p. 330). Vaillant's research highlighted the role of these protective factors in healthy aging. The more factors the subjects had in place, the better the odds they had for longer, happier lives.

The study showed that the role of genetics and long-lived ancestors proved less important to longevity than the level of satisfaction with relationships in midlife, now recognized as a good predictor of healthy aging. The research also debunked the idea that people's personalities "set like plaster" by age 30 and cannot be changed.

"Those who were clearly train wrecks when they were in their 20s turned out to be wonderful octogenarians," he said. "On the other hand, alcoholism and major depression could take people who started life as stars and leave them at the end of their lives as train wrecks." George Valliant.

The study's fourth director, Waldinger has expanded research to the wives and children of the original men. Waldinger hopes to expand this second-generation study into the third and fourth generations. "It will probably never be replicated," he said of the lengthy research, adding that there is yet more to learn.

"We're trying to see how people manage stress, whether their bodies are in a sort of chronic 'fight or flight' mode," Waldinger said. "We want to find out how it is that a difficult childhood reaches across decades to break down the body in middle age and later." (Mineo, 2017, p.103)

Asked what lessons he has learned from the study, Waldinger, who is a Zen priest, said he practices meditation daily and invests time and energy in his relationships, more than before.

"It's easy to get isolated, to get caught up in work and not remembering, 'Oh, I haven't seen these friends in a long time," Waldinger said. "So, I try to pay more attention to my relationships than I used to." (Mineo, 2017)

According to Gregoire (2013), below are five lessons from the Harvard Longitudinal Grant Study to apply to your own pursuit of a happier and more meaningful life:

Love Is Really All That Matters

It may seem obvious, but that doesn't make it any less true: Love is key to a happy and fulfilling life. As Vaillant puts it, there are two pillars of happiness. "One is love," he writes. "The other is finding a way of coping with life that does not push love away."

Vaillant has said that the study's most important finding is that the only thing that matters in life is relationships. A man could have a successful career, money and good physical health, but without supportive, loving relationships, he wouldn't be happy ("Happiness is only the cart; love is the horse."). (Gregoire, 2013)

It's About More than Money and Power

The Grant Study's findings echoed those of other studies -- that acquiring more money and power doesn't correlate to greater happiness. That's not to say money or traditional career success don't matter. But they're small parts of a much larger picture -- and while they may loom large for us in the moment, they diminish in importance when viewed in the context of a full life.

"We found that contentment in the late 70s was not even suggestively associated with parental social class or even the man's own income," says Vaillant. "In terms of achievement, the only thing that matters is that you be content at your work." (Gregoire, 2013)

Regardless of How We Begin Life, We Can All Become Happier

A man named Godfrey Minot Camille went into the Grant study with fairly bleak prospects for life satisfaction: He had the lowest rating for future stability of all the subjects and he had previously attempted suicide. But at the end of his life, he was one of the happiest. Why? As Vaillant explains, "He spent his life searching for love." (Gregoire, 2013)

Connection Is Crucial

"Joy is connection," Vaillant says. "The more areas in your life you can make connection, the better."

The study found strong relationships to be far and away the strongest predictor of life satisfaction. And in terms of career satisfaction, too, feeling connected to one's work was far more important than making money or achieving traditional success.

"The conclusion of the study, not in a medical but in a psychological sense, is that connection is the whole shooting match," says Vaillant.

As life goes on, connections become even more important. The Grant Study provides strong support for the growing body of research that has linked social ties with longevity, lower stress levels and improved overall well-being. (Gregoire, 2013)

Challenges—and the Perspective They Give You—Can Make You Happier

The journey from immaturity to maturity, says Vaillant, is a sort of movement from narcissism to connection, and a big part of this shift has to do with the way we deal with challenges.

Coping mechanisms -- "the capacity to make gold out of shit," as Vaillant puts it -- have a significant effect on social support and overall well-being. The secret is replacing narcissism, a single-minded focus on one's own emotional oscillations and perceived problems, with mature coping defenses, Vaillant explains, citing Mother Teresa and Beethoven as examples.

"Mother Teresa had a perfectly terrible childhood, and her inner spiritual life was very painful," says Vaillant. "But she had a highly successful life by caring about other people. Creative expression is another way to productively deal with challenges and achieve meaning and well-being.

"The secret of Beethoven being able to cope with misery through his art was when he wrote 'Ode to Joy,'" says Vaillant. "Beethoven was able to make connection with his music." (Gregoire, 2013)

Here are some notes from Harvard Health Publishing: Harvard Medical School (2010) on the importance of social relationships:

- The benefits of strong relationships: Social relationships not only give us pleasure, they also influence our long-term health in ways as powerful as quality sleep, good nutrition, and not smoking. People who have satisfying relationships with family, friends and their community are happier, have fewer health problems, and live longer.
- People without strong relationships experience higher rates of depression and later-life cognitive decline, as well as increased mortality. The mortality risk of poor relationships is roughly equal to that of smoking 15 cigarettes a day. This is greater than the risk involving obesity and physical inactivity.
- What makes social connections healthful? Social connectedness helps relieve harmful levels of stress which can adversely affect coronary arteries, gut function, insulin regulation, and the immune system. Caring behaviors also trigger the release of stress-reducing hormones.
- Social support can involve a range of activities such as offers of help or advice, and expressions of affection, and the benefits extend to both the giver and receiver of support.

So, caring involvement with others may be one of the easiest health strategies to access since it requires no special equipment and is inexpensive.

"Social Relations & Health: A Flashpoint for Health Policy" (Umberson & Montez, 2010)

This study reviewed the research on the impact of social relationships on mental health, health behavior, physical health, and mortality risk, and highlights policy implications suggested by the research. Umberson and Montez's (2010) five key research findings were: 1) social relationships have significant effects on health; 2) social relationships affect health through behavioral, psychological, and physiological pathways; 3) relationships have costs and benefits for health; 4) relationships shape health outcomes throughout life and have a cumulative impact on health over time; and 5) the cost and benefits of social relationships are not distributed equally in the population.

Three Important Ways Social Relationships Benefit Health: Behavioral, Psychological, and Physiological

Social relationships benefit health in three broad ways: behavioral, psychological, and physiological:

Behavioral: Health behaviors explain 40% of premature mortality as well as substantial disability in the United States. Health behaviors such as exercise, healthy nutrition, and adherence to medical regimens, promote health and prevent illness, while other behaviors, such as smoking, excessive weight gain, drug use, and heavy alcohol consumption undermine health (Umberson & Montez, 2010). Social ties influence health behavior, in part, because they influence, or control, our health habits (a spouse may monitor, inhibit, or facilitate behaviors that promote a partner's health). Religious ties also seem to influence health behaviors, in part, through social control. Social ties provide information and create norms that influence health habits (Umberson & Montez, 2010).

- **Psychological**: Psychological mechanisms that promote health behaviors include social support, personal control, symbolic meaning and norms, and mental health (Umberson & Montez, 2010).
- **Social support**: The sense that one is cared for, loved and listened to. Many studies confirm the benefits of social support on mental and physical health (Cohen, 2004; Uchino, 2004). Social support may enhance health by reducing the impact of stress, and fostering a sense of meaning and purpose in life. Supportive social ties also have physiological reactions that promote health such as reduce blood pressure, heart rate, and stress hormone levels (Umberson & Montez, 2010).

- **Personal control**: Personal control refers to beliefs that one has at least some control of life outcomes through one's actions and behaviors. Social support may enhance these beliefs (Umberson & Montez, 2010).

- **Symbolic meaning and norms**: Meaning attached to marriage, and relationships with children, may foster healthy behaviors/lifestyle (Umberson & Montez, 2010).

- **Mental health**: The emotional support of social ties enhances psychological wellbeing, which, in turn, helps to reduce risky behaviors associated with poor health. Mental health is essential for overall health. Mental illness is the leading cause of disability in both low and high income countries (Umberson & Montez, 2010). Mental disorders account for 37% of the total years of healthy life lost due to disability (Mathers et al., 2010).

- **Physiological**: Supportive social ties benefit immune, endocrine, and cardiovascular functioning. Social support reduces physiological responses, such as cardiovascular reactivity to both anticipated and existing stressors (Umberson & Montez, 2010).

Cumulative Advantages and Disadvantages of Social Relationships

While social support may have many benefits, some social relationships can be extremely stressful. For example, poor marital quality has been associated with weakened immune and endocrine systems as well as depression. Relationship stress undermines a sense of personal control and mental health, both of which, are associated with poorer physical health. Relationships with unhealthy risk-taking peers may contribute to increased alcohol consumption, drug use or becoming obese. Caring for one's social ties may also involve personal health costs. For example, providing care to a sick or impaired spouse may strain the health of the provider.

Research Driven Policy Recommendations

There is a solid research base that establishes a causal relationship between social support on health. This research provides the rationale for health policy that seeks to protect and promote social support and the health benefits that result. The Umberson and Montez (2010) study concludes with the following five public policy foundational statements:

1. Social ties affect mental health, physical health, health behaviors, and mortality risks.
2. Social ties are a potential resource that can be harnessed to promote populations health.
3. Social ties are a resource that should be protected as well as promoted.
4. Social ties benefit health beyond target individuals by influencing the health of others throughout social networks.
5. Social ties have both immediate (mental health, health behaviors) and long-term, cumulative effects on health (e.g., physical health, mortality), and thus represent opportunities for short-and long-term investment in population health. (p. 8).

APA Psychology Help Center: Strengthen Your Support System to Manage Stress

The American Psychological Association (APA) Help Center publishes articles on a variety of health issues, such as strengthening your social support system to manage stress. In 2016, the APA published a "2015 Stress in America" survey of American adults, and found overall stress levels at 5.1 on a 10 point scale, where 10 = great deal of stress, and 1 = little or no stress). Twenty-four percent reported ratings of 8 or higher (considered extreme stress). Social support acts as a protective factor against extreme stress. This same survey found the average stress level for those with social support to be 5.0 versus 6.3 for those without social support (APA, 2016).

Loneliness has been associated with a wide range of health problems including high blood pressure, diminished immunity, cardiovascular disease, and cognitive decline. Low levels of social support have also been linked to increased death from cardiovascular disease, infectious disease, and cancer.

The good news is that there are ways to seek out social support and nurture supportive relationships. Many people go about connecting with others to increase their social support by choosing to be around people who share a common interest or purpose (for example, joining a gym or look for an exercise buddy, getting involved in a hobby to connect with others with same interest, volunteering with others, joining a book club/discussion group/movie group). Having one or two close and supportive friends is at least as valuable to emotional health as having a large group of friendly acquaintances or more shallow friendships. However, having social support from several close and supportive friends could be the best of both worlds. What are some other ways that you have found to connect with others and build your social support network?

Take a look at "My Social Support Network" and list as many people as you can for each category. You may not have anyone for some categories, which is to be expected. After you complete your network list, reflect on what pleases you most and what you might want to do to increase your network.

My Social Support Network

Who do you go to when you need…

Support, validation, caring: _____, _____, _____

Motivation to exercise: _____, _____, _____

Advice, problem-solving: _____, _____, _____

Play-mates/fun: _____, _____, _____

Support for eating healthy: _____, _____, _____

Other: _____, _____, _____

One thing I am surprised by:

One thing I am pleased about:

One thing I see I would like to do:

I would like to wrap-up this chapter with one other scale used to measure your social support level. The Lubben Social Network Scale (LSNS) is one of the widely-used instruments to assess perceived social support received from family and friends, and has been commonly applied in social and health care research. James Lubben is Professor Emeritus at UCLA where he taught for 20 years and was Associate Dean and Department Chair. He was also Professor Emeritus at Boston College where he was the Louise McMahon Ahearn Endowed Professor in Social Work for 15 years. He has published over 125 peer reviewed articles and chapters and edited 7 books. He has been a principal investigator or collaborator on over $35 million (direct costs) of research and training grants. The primary aim of his research examines social isolation as a behavioral health risk among older populations. To carry out this research, he developed the LSNS, an abbreviated measure designed for both research and clinical use among older populations. The LSNS has been translated into many languages and employed in studies throughout the world. Scores on the LSNS have been associated with a wide array of health indicators including mortality, morbidity, psychological distress and loneliness, cognitive impairment, and health care use. Rate your social connectedness using the LSNS.

Lubben Social Network Scale

Scoring: The total score is calculated by finding the sum of the all items. For the LSNS-R, the score ranges between 0 and 60, with a higher score indicating more social engagement. References:

Lubben, J. (1988). Assessing social networks among elderly populations. *Family & Community Health: The Journal of Health Promotion & Maintenance, 11,* 42–52.

Less Social Engagement More Social Engagement						
All questions	0	1	2	3	4	5

Lubben Social Network Scale

FAMILY: Considering the people to whom you are related by birth, marriage, adoption, etc...

1. How many relatives do you see or hear from at least once a month?
   0 = none 1 = one 2 = two 3 = three or four 4 = five thru eight 5 = nine or more

2. How often do you see or hear from the relative with whom you have the most contact?
   0 = less than monthly 1 = monthly 2 = few times a month 3 = weekly 4 = few times a week 5 = daily

3. How many relatives do you feel at ease with that you can talk about private matters?
   0 = none 1 = one 2 = two 3 = three or four 4 = five thru eight 5 = nine or more

4. How many relatives do you feel close to such that you could call on them for help?
   0 = none 1 = one 2 = two 3 = three or four 4 = five thru eight 5 = nine or more

5. When one of your relatives has an important decision to make, how often do they talk to you about it?
   0 = never 1 = seldom 2 = sometimes 3 = often 4 = very often 5 = always

6. How often is one of your relatives available for you to talk to when you have an important decision to make?
   0 = never 1 = seldom 2 = sometimes 3 = often 4 = very often 5 = always

FRIENDSHIPS: Considering all of your friends including those who live in your neighborhood...

7. How many of your friends do you see or hear from at least once a month?
   0 = none 1 = one 2 = two 3 = three or four 4 = five thru eight 5 = nine or more

8. How often do you see or hear from the friend with whom you have the most contact?
   0 = less than monthly 1 = monthly 2 = few times a month 3 = weekly 4 = few times a week 5 = daily

9. How many friends do you feel at ease with that you can talk about private matters?

  0 = none 1 = one 2 = two 3 = three or four 4 = five thru eight 5 = nine or more

10. How many friends do you feel close to such that you could call on them for help?

  0 = none 1 = one 2 = two 3 = three or four 4 = five thru eight 5 = nine or more

11. When one of your friends has an important decision to make, how often do they talk to you about it?

  0 = never 1 = seldom 2 = sometimes 3 = often 4 = very often 5 = always

12. How often is one of your friends available for you to talk to when you have an important decision to make?

  0 = never 1 = seldom 2 = sometimes 3 = often 4 = very often 5 = always

Reflection on my social network scale score:

I was surprised that:

I was pleased about:

One thing I see I would like to do:

References

Adler, A. (1964). *Social interest: A challenge to mankind.* (J. Linton & R. Vaughn, Ed. & Trans.). Capricorn Books. (Original work published 1933)

American Psychological Association. (2016). *Stress in America: The impact of discrimination.* https://www.apa.org/news/press/releases/stress/2015/impact-of-discrimination.pdf

Brigman, G., Villares, E., & Webb, L. (2018). *Looking good/feeling good* [Infographic]. Evidence-based school counseling: A student success approach. Routledge.

Cohen, S. (2004). *Social relationships and health.* American Psychologist, 59(8), 676–684. https://doi.org/10.1037/0003-066X.59.8.676

Crooks, V., Lubben, J., Petitti, D., Little, D., & Chiu, V. (2008). Social network, cognitive function, and dementia incidence among elderly women. *American Journal of Public Health, 98*(7): 1221–1227. https://doi.org/10.2105/AJPH.2007.115923

Fromm, E. (2019). *The art of loving.* Harper Perennial Modern Classis.

Gregoire, C. (2013). The 75-Year study that found the secrets to a fulfilling life. *Huffington Post.* https://www.huffpost.com/entry/how-this-harvard-psycholo_n_3727229

Gottman, J. (2014). *What predicts divorce?: The relationship between marital processes and marital outcomes.* Psychology Press.

Gottman, J., & DeClaire, J. (2001). *The relationship cure: A five-step guide for building better connections with family, friends, and lovers.* Crown.

Gottman, J., & Silver, N. (1999). *The seven principles for making marriage work: A practical guide from the country's foremost relationship expert.* Harmony.

Harvard Health Publishing Harvard Medical School. (2010). *The health benefits of strong relationships.* Harvard Health Publishing Harvard Medical School: Trusted Advice for a Healthier Life. https://www.health.harvard.edu/newsletter_article/the-health-benefits-of-strong-relationships Lubben, J. (1988). Assessing social networks among elderly populations. *Family & Community Health: The Journal of Health Promotion & Maintenance, 11*(3), 42–52.

Lubben, J. (2018). Addressing social isolation as a potent killer! *Public Policy & Aging Report, 27*(4), 136–138. https://doi.org/10.1093/ppar/prx026

Lubben, J. E., Blozik, E., Gillmann, G., Iliffe, S., con Rentein Kruse, W., Beck, J. C., & Stuck, A. E. (2006). Performance of an abbreviated version of the Lubben Social Network Scale among three European community-dwelling older adult populations. *The Gerontologist, 46*(4):503–513. https://doi.org/ 10.1093/geront/46.4.503

Massachusetts General Hospital & Harvard Medical School. (2015). *Harvard Second Generation Study.* Retrieved May 1, 2020, from https://www.adultdevelopmentstudy.org/

Mathers, C., Lopez, A., & Murray, C. (2006). The burden of disease and mortality by condition: Data, methods, and results for 2001. In A.D. Lopez, C. D. Mathers, M. Ezzati, D. T. Jamison, & C. J. Murray (Eds.), *Global Burden of Disease and Risk Factors* (2006, pp. 45–240). The World Bank and Oxford University Press.

Messerly, J. (2014). Summary of Erich Fromm's, The art of loving. *Reason and Meaning: Philosophical Reflections on Life, Death, and the Meaning of Life.* https://reasonandmeaning. com/2014/07/29/the-art-of-loving/

Mineo, L. (2017). Good genes are nice, but joy is better. *The Harvard Gazette.* https://news. harvard.edu/gazette/story/2017/04/over-nearly-80-years-harvard-study-has-been-showing-how-to-live-a-healthy-and-happy-life/

Robin, M. (n.d.). *The gifts of love, time, and attention.* Dr. Michelle Robin. https://www. drmichellerobin.com/

Uchino, B. (2004). *Social support and physical health: Understanding the health consequences of relationships.* Yale University Press.

Umberson, D., & Montez, J. K. (2010). Social relationships and health: A flashpoint for health policy. *Journal of Health and Social Behavior, 51*(Suppl), S54–S66. https://doi.org/10.1177/0022146510383501

Valliant, G. E. (1998). *Adaptation to life.* Harvard University Press. (Original work published in 1977)

Valliant, G. E. (2002). *Aging well: Surprising guideposts to a happier life from the landmark Harvard Study of Adult Aging.* Little, Brown and Company.

Valliant, G. E. (2012). *Triumphs of experience: The men of the Harvard Grant Study.* Belknap Press of Harvard University Press.

Valliant, G. E., & Mukami, K. (2001). Successful again. *The American Journal of Psychiatry, 158*(6):839–47. https://doi.org/10.1176/appi.ajp.158.6.839

Waldinger, R. (2019). *What makes a good life? Lessons from the longest study on happiness* [Video]. TED Conferences. https://www.ted.com/talks/robert_waldinger_what_makes_a_good_life_lessons_ from_the_longest_study_on_happiness/discussion?language=en

CHAPTER 5

REST/SLEEP

"This silent sleep loss epidemic is the greatest public health challenge
we face in the twenty-first century in developed nations."
—Matthew Walker, *Why We Sleep: Unlocking the Power of Sleep and Dreams*

Chapter Highlights:

- Stanford Sleep Research Pioneer, William Dement
- *Why We Sleep*, Matthew Walker
- NIH 12 Tips for Quality Sleep
- National Sleep Foundation
- Deep Sleep and Clearing Out Brain Toxins
- Top 10 Sleep Myths
- Guidelines for Insomnia
- Online Resources

LOOKING GOOD / FEELING GOOD

5. Rest

Liquids: ▲ water & milk ▲ juice ▼ sodas
Solids: ▲ fruits & veggies ▼ sweets & chips

	Week 1	Week 2	Week 3	Week 4	Week 5	Week 6	Week 7	Week 8
5	▲▼	▲▼	▲▼	▲▼	▲▼	▲▼	▲▼	▲▼

Circle the up triangle if you improved even a little this past week.
Think about your week.

Did you get even a little closer to the recommended 8-9 hours of
sleep this week?

65

Rest/Sleep is the last of five components that affect our energy and mood on our Looking Good/Feeling Good (LGFG) chart, but don't think it is less important than any of the other four. Sleep is one of the most important, but least understood, contributors to our health and wellbeing. Sleep helps us learn and make good decisions. It allows us to recalibrate our emotions, boost our immune system, and regulate our metabolism and appetite.

In this chapter, I want to share some of my favorite sources for research-based recommendations related to this sleep/rest. To start, I have to mention William Dement, MD, who is considered the father of sleep research and founder of the Sleep Research Center at Stanford University. He is a leading authority on sleep, sleep deprivation, and the diagnosis and treatment of sleep disorders, such as sleep apnea and narcolepsy.

One of my top sleep resources is Matthew Walker's, PhD, excellent book, *Why We Sleep: Unlocking the Power of Sleep and Dreams.*

Matthew Walker is Professor of Neuroscience and Psychology at UC Berkley, Director of the Center for Human Sleep Science, and former Professor of Psychiatry at Harvard University. As a recognized expert in sleep science, he has appeared on 60 minutes, Nova, BBC News, and NPR Science Friday. According to Walker (2018):

> The sleep loss epidemic is the greatest public health challenge we face in the twenty-first century in developed nations. If we wish to avoid the suffocating noose of sleep neglect, the premature death it inflicts, and the sickening health it invites, a radical shift in our personal, cultural, professional, and societal appreciation of sleep must occur. I believe it is time to reclaim our right to a full night's sleep, without embarrassment or the damaging stigma of laziness. In doing so, we can be reunited with that most powerful elixir of wellness and vitality, dispensed through every conceivable biological pathway. Then we may remember what it feels like to be truly awake during the day, infused with the very deepest plenitude of being. (p. 340)

Here are the National Institutes of Health's (NIH's) 12 tips for improved sleep, which are provided in Walker's book. As you read these recommendations, compare them to other tips in this chapter and to additional recommendations you have discovered, and decide on the ones most helpful to you. Write these down and begin to follow them every day to maximize your sleep quality. Sleep is too important to not have a research-based plan to follow regularly.

National Institute of Health's 12 Tips for Improving Quantity and Quality of Your Sleep

1. Stick to a sleep schedule. Go to bed and wake up at the same time each day. Sleeping later on weekends will not fully make up for lack of sleep during the week and will make it harder to wake up early Monday morning. If there is only one piece of advice you take away from these twelve tips, this should be it.

2. Exercise is great, but do not do it too late in the day. Try to exercise at least thirty minutes on most days but not later than 2–3 hours before bedtime.

3. Avoid caffeine and nicotine. Coffee, colas, certain teas, and chocolate contain the stimulant caffeine, and its effect can take as long as eight hours to wear off fully. Therefore, a cup of coffee in the late afternoon can make it hard for you to fall asleep at night. Nicotine is also a stimulant, often causing smokers to sleep only very lightly. In addition, smokers often wake up too early in the morning because of nicotine withdrawal.

4. Avoid alcohol drinks before bed. Having a nightcap or alcoholic beverage before sleep may help you relax, but heavy use robs you of your REM sleep, keeping you from the lighter stages of sleep. Heavy alcohol ingestion may also contribute to impairment in breathing at night. You also tend to wake up in the middle of the night when the effects of the alcohol have worn off.

5. Avoid large meals and beverages late at night. A light snack is okay, but a large meal can cause indigestion, which interferes with sleep. Drinking too many fluids at night can cause frequent awakenings to urinate.

6. If possible, avoid medicines that delay or disrupt sleep. Some commonly prescribed heart, blood pressure, or asthma medications, as well as some over the counter and herbal remedies for coughs, colds or allergies, can disrupt sleep patterns. If you have trouble sleeping, talk to your health care provider or pharmacist to see whether any drugs you're taking might be contributing to your insomnia and ask whether they can be taken at other times during the day or early in the evening.

7. Don't take naps after 3 p.m. Naps can help you make up for lost sleep, but late afternoon naps can make it harder to fall asleep at night.

8. Relax before bed. Don't overschedule your day so that no time is left for unwinding. A relaxing activity, such as reading or listening to music, should be part of your bedtime ritual.

9. Take a hot bath before bed. The drop-in temperature after getting out of the bath may help you feel sleepy, and the bath can help you relax and slow down so you're more ready to sleep.

10. Dark bedroom, cool bedroom, gadget free bedroom. Get rid of anything in your bedroom that might distract you from sleep, such as noises, bright lights, an uncomfortable bed, or warm temperatures. You sleep better if the temperature in the room is kept on the cool side. A TV, cell phone, or computer in the bedroom can be a distraction and deprive you of needed sleep. Having a comfortable mattress and pillow can help promote a good night's sleep. Individuals who have insomnia often watch the clock. Turn the clock's face out of view so you don't worry about the time while trying to fall asleep.

11. Have the right sun exposure. Daylight is the key to regulating daily sleep patterns. Try to get outside in natural sunlight for at least thirty minutes each day. If possible, wake up with the sunlight or use very bright lights in the morning. Sleep experts recommend that, if you have a problem falling asleep, you should get an hour of exposure to morning sunlight and turn down the lights before bedtime.

12. Don't lie in bed awake. If you find yourself still awake after staying in bed for more than twenty minutes or if you are starting to feel anxious or worried, get up and do some relaxing activity until you feel sleepy. The anxiety of not being able to sleep can make it harder to fall asleep. (Walker, 2018, p. 341–342)

James B. Maas, PhD, is another internationally recognized authority on sleep and performance. He has served as a Stephen H. Weiss Presidential Fellow, Professor and past Chairman of Psychology, as well as a professor in the graduate fields of Education and Communication at Cornell University. He has authored several books on sleep including: *Power Sleep: The Revolutionary Program that Prepares Your Mind for Peak Performance*, and *Sleep for Success! Everything You Must Know About Sleep But are Too Tired to Ask*.

Maas has developed the following "Four Keys to Sleeping Well." Which ones do you currently follow, and which ones are you willing to try?

1. **Determine your Personal Sleep Quotient (or PSQ) and meet it nightly**.
   Your PSQ is essentially how much sleep YOU need on a given night. The range is likely to be between 7.5 hours and 9 hours. To discover your personal PSQ, to go to bed at a time that will give you 8 hours of sleep. If you can't wake up without an alarm feeling refreshed, give yourself 15 more minutes of sleep until you can.

2. **Go to bed at the same time every night and wake up naturally at the same time every morning, including weekends.**
   Big Idea: BE CONSISTENT. 7 days a week, 365 days a year. Don't sleep in on weekends. That basically gives you jet lag and leads to really cranky Monday mornings. Are you consistent or are you all over the place? *"Regularity is vital for setting and stabilizing your body's biological clock."*

3. **Get your required amount of sleep in one continuous block.**
   Of course, it's not always possible to get one long chunk of sleep, but that's the target. *"Six hours of continuous sleep are often more restorative than eight hours of fragmented sleep."*

4. **Make up for lost sleep as soon as possible.**
   We're building up a sleep debt with every hour we're awake. Basically, for every 2 hours we're up, we owe 1 hour of sleep. If we build up too much debt, we will crash. So, if you skimp one night, try to make it up the next night—but do it by going to bed earlier rather than sleeping in later! (And, naps can be helpful but do them earlier so you don't disrupt your sleep that night.) (Maas et al., 2008, p. 74–78)

One of the most surprising and exciting things I have learned about sleep involves how our brain is washed each night during deep restorative sleep. A brief explanation is found below from NPR's *All Things Considered* segment, "Our Brains Sweep Themselves Clean of Toxins During Sleep," by Jon Hamilton (2013):

While the brain sleeps, it clears out harmful toxins, a process that may reduce the risk of Alzheimer's, researchers say. During sleep, the flow of cerebrospinal fluid in the brain increases dramatically, washing away harmful waste proteins that build up between brain cells during waking hours. "It's like a dishwasher," says Dr. Maiken Nedergaard, a professor of neurosurgery at the University of Rochester and an author of the study involving mice in *Science.*

The results appear to offer the best explanation yet of why animals and people need sleep. If this proves to be true in humans as well, it could help explain a mysterious association between sleep disorders and brain diseases, including Alzheimer's. Nedergaard and a team of scientists discovered the cleaning process while studying the brains of sleeping mice.

The team discovered that this increased flow was possible in part because when mice went to sleep, their brain cells actually shrank, making it easier for fluid to circulate. When an animal woke up, the brain cells enlarged again and the flow between cells slowed to a trickle. "It's almost like opening and closing a faucet," Nedergaard says. "It's that dramatic."

Nedergaard's team, which is funded by the National Institute of Neurological Disorders and Stroke, had previously shown that this fluid was carrying away waste products that build up in the spaces between brain cells.

The brain-cleaning process has been observed in rats and baboons, but not yet in humans, Nedergaard says. Even so, it could offer a new way of understanding human brain diseases including Alzheimer's. That's because one of the waste products removed from the brain during sleep is beta amyloid, the substance that forms sticky plaques associated with the disease.

That's probably not a coincidence, Nedergaard says. "Isn't it interesting that Alzheimer's and all other diseases associated with dementia, are linked to sleep disorders," she says.

The study was co-led by UC Berkeley neuroscientists Bryce Mander and William Jagust, a leading expert on Alzheimer's disease. The team has received a major National

Institutes of Health grant to conduct a longitudinal study to test their hypothesis that sleep is an early warning sign or biomarker of Alzheimer's disease. (Hamilton, 2013).

The following is an excerpt from a *UC Berkley News, Mind & Body Research* article, "Poor Sleep Linked to Toxic Buildup of Alzheimer's Protein, Memory Loss," by Yasmin Anwar (2015):

Sleep may be a missing piece in the Alzheimer's disease puzzle.

UC Berkeley scientists have found compelling evidence that poor sleep – particularly a deficit of the deep, restorative slumber needed to hit the save button on memories – is a channel through which the beta-amyloid protein believed to trigger Alzheimer's disease attacks the brain's long-term memory.

"Our findings reveal a new pathway through which Alzheimer's disease may cause memory decline later in life," said UC Berkeley neuroscience professor Matthew Walker, senior author of the study published in the journal *Nature Neuroscience*.

Excessive deposits of beta-amyloid are key suspects in the pathology of Alzheimer's disease, a virulent form of dementia caused by the gradual death of brain cells. An unprecedented wave of aging baby boomers is expected to make Alzheimer's disease, which has been diagnosed in more than 40 million people, one of the world's fastest-growing and most debilitating public health concerns.

The good news about the findings, Walker said, is that poor sleep is potentially treatable and can be enhanced through exercise, behavioral therapy and even electrical stimulation that amplifies brain waves during sleep, a technology that has been used successfully in young adults to increase their overnight memory.

"This discovery offers hope," he said. "Sleep could be a novel therapeutic target for fighting back against memory impairment in older adults and even those with dementia."

The study was co-led by UC Berkeley neuroscientists Bryce Mander and William Jagust, a leading expert on Alzheimer's disease. The team has received a major National

Institutes of Health grant to conduct a longitudinal study to test their hypothesis that sleep is an early warning sign or biomarker of Alzheimer's disease.

While most research in this area has depended on animal subjects, this latest study has the advantage of human subjects recruited by William Jagust, a professor with joint appointments at UC Berkeley's Helen Wills Neuroscience Institute, the School of Public Health and the Lawrence Berkeley National Laboratory.

"Over the past few years, the links between sleep, beta-amyloid, memory, and Alzheimer's disease have been growing stronger," Jagust said. "Our study shows that this beta-amyloid deposition may lead to a vicious cycle in which sleep is further disturbed and memory impaired."

Using a powerful combination of brain imaging and other diagnostic tools on 26 older adults who have not been diagnosed with dementia, researchers looked for the link between bad sleep, poor memory and the toxic accumulation of beta-amyloid proteins.

"The data we've collected are very suggestive that there's a causal link," said Mander, lead author of the study and a postdoctoral researcher in the Sleep and Neuroimaging Laboratory directed by Walker. "If we intervene to improve sleep, perhaps we can break that causal chain." (Anwar, 2015)

For more information: http://www.stonehearthnewsletters.com/alzheimers-tied-to-lack-of-sleep-in-new-uc-berkeley-study/alzheimers/#sthash.c5giLFeP.N4EEWy6e.dpuf

I want to wrap up this chapter with some excerpts from the U.S. Department of Health and Human Services's (HHS's) comprehensive guide, "Your Guide to Healthy Sleep," that I find very helpful, which includes "Top 10 Sleep Myths" and guidelines to deal with insomnia. Finally, I list several authoritative resources to help you become well-informed about this important topic. Below is an excerpt from an NIH (2006) news release, "NIH Offers New Comprehensive Guide to Healthy Sleep":

In today's "24/7" society, many people cut back on sleep to squeeze in more time for work, family obligations, and other activities. But skimping on sleep can be harmful.

A comprehensive handbook from the National Heart, Lung, and Blood Institute (NHLBI) of the National Institutes of Health (NIH) explains that sleep is not merely "down time" when the brain shuts off and the body rests.

"Our brains are very active during sleep, and research has shown that adequate sleep is important to our overall health, safety, and performance," notes Michael Twery, PhD, acting director of NHLBI's National Center on Sleep Disorders Research. "Scientists also have a better understanding of how a chronic lack of sleep or an untreated sleep disorder can impair health. Like good nutrition and physical activity, adequate sleep is critical for continued good health."

"Your Guide to Healthy Sleep" provides the latest science-based information about sleep in an easy-to-understand format. The 60-page handbook describes how and why we sleep, and offers tips for getting adequate sleep, such as sticking to a sleep schedule, relaxing before going to bed, and using daylight or bright light to help you adjust to jet lag and shift work schedules.

Sleep disorders such as insomnia (trouble falling asleep or staying asleep, or unrefreshing sleep), sleep apnea (brief periods of pauses in breathing or shallow breathing while you are sleeping), restless legs syndrome (an almost irresistible urge to move the legs that can make it difficult to fall asleep or stay asleep), and narcolepsy (excessive and overwhelming daytime sleepiness despite adequate nighttime sleep) are also described with information on diagnosis and treatment. In addition, a sample sleep diary helps readers track their sleep-related habits.

Sleep needs vary from person to person, and they change throughout the lifecycle. Newborns sleep between 16 and 18 hours a day, and children in preschool sleep between 10 and 12 hours a day. School-aged children and teens need at least 9 hours of sleep a day. Research suggests that adults — including seniors — need at least 7 to 8 hours of sleep each day to be well rested and to perform at their best.

Studies have linked sleep to our ability to learn, create memories, and solve problems. Sleep has also been tied to mood. Without enough sleep, a person has trouble focusing, and responding quickly — a potentially dangerous combination, such as when driving. In addition, mounting evidence links a chronic lack of sleep with an increased risk for developing obesity, diabetes, cardiovascular disease, and infections. (NIH, 2006)

Rapid Eye Movement (REM) sleep plays an important role in our overall sleep health. REM sleep is when dreaming occurs. Dreaming helps information processing and inspires creativity and promotes problem solving. Deep REM sleep strengthens individual memories. REM sleep fuses and blends memories together in abstract and highly novel ways. During REM sleep, your brain cogitates vast swaths of acquired knowledge and then extracts overarching rules and commonalities, "the gist." This process is important to problem-solving. To support quality REM sleep, avoid the nightcap—alcohol is one of the most powerful suppressors of REM sleep. Alcohol infused sleep is fragmented sleep, not continuous sleep and as a result not restorative

The quality of sleep is also important. How well rested you are, and how well you function the next day, depend on your total sleep time and how much of the various stages of sleep you get each night. Yet, each year an estimated 70 million adult Americans have some type of sleep problem. Returning to the NIH (2006) news release:

"Although there are times during the day when we are naturally likely to feel drowsy, in many cases, sleepiness is a sign that something is amiss," adds Twery. "The handbook offers several ideas to help you improve your sleep, but if you feel that you regularly have problems breathing during sleep, wake up unrefreshed after a full night's sleep, or frequently feel very sleepy during the day, you should see your doctor to find out if you could have a sleep disorder."

Below are some myths about sleep from the U.S. Department of Health and Human Services's (2011) 60-page handbook, "Your Guide to Healthy Sleep," which I want to be sure you know about:

Top Ten Sleep Myths

Myth 1: Sleep is a time when your body and brain shut down for rest and relaxation. No evidence shows that any major organ (including the brain) or regulatory system in the body shuts down during sleep. Some physiological processes actually become more active while you sleep. For example, secretion of certain hormones is boosted, and activity of the pathways in the brain linked to learning and memory increases.

Myth 2: Getting just 1 hour less sleep per night than needed will not have any effect on your daytime functioning. This lack of sleep may not make you noticeably sleepy during the day. But even slightly less sleep can affect your ability to think properly and respond quickly, and it can impair your cardiovascular health and energy balance as well as your body's ability to fight infections, particularly if lack of sleep continues. If you consistently do not get enough sleep, a sleep debt builds up that you can never repay. This sleep debt affects your health and quality of life and makes you feel tired during the day.

Myth 3: Your body adjusts quickly to different sleep schedules. Your biological clock makes you most alert during the daytime and least alert at night. Thus, even if you work the night shift, you will naturally feel sleepy when nighttime comes. Most people can reset their biological clock, but only by appropriately timed cues—and even then, by 1–2 hours per day at best. Consequently, it can take more than a week to adjust to a substantial change in your sleep–wake cycle—for example, when traveling across several time zones or switching from working the day shift to the night shift.

Myth 4: People need less sleep as they get older. Older people don't need less sleep, but they may get less sleep or find their sleep less refreshing. That's because as people age, the quality of their sleep changes. Older people are also more likely to have insomnia or other medical conditions that disrupt their sleep.

Myth 5: Extra sleep for one night can cure you of problems with excessive daytime fatigue. Not only is the quantity of sleep important, but also the quality of sleep. Some people sleep 8 or 9 hours a night but don't feel well rested when they wake up because the quality of their sleep is poor. A number of sleep disorders and other medical conditions affect the quality of sleep. Sleeping more won't lessen the daytime sleepiness these disorders or conditions cause. However, many of these disorders or conditions can be treated effectively with changes in behavior or with medical therapies. Additionally, one night of increased sleep may not correct multiple nights of inadequate sleep.

Myth 6: You can make up for lost sleep during the week by sleeping more on the weekends. Although this sleeping pattern will help you feel more rested, it will not completely make up for the lack of sleep or correct your sleep debt. This pattern also will not necessarily make up for impaired performance during the week or the physical problems that can result from not sleeping enough. Furthermore, sleeping later on the weekends can affect your biological clock, making it much harder to go to sleep at the right time on Sunday nights and get up early on Monday mornings.

Myth 7: Naps are a waste of time. Although naps are no substitute for a good night's sleep, they can be restorative and help counter some of the effects of not getting enough sleep at night. Naps can actually help you learn how to do certain tasks quicker. But avoid taking naps later than 3 p.m., particularly if you have trouble falling asleep at night, as late naps can make it harder for you to fall asleep when you go to bed. Also, limit your naps to no longer than 20 minutes, because longer naps will make it harder to wake up and get back in the swing of things. If you take more than one or two planned or unplanned naps during the day, you may have a sleep disorder that should be treated.

Myth 8: Snoring is a normal part of sleep. Snoring during sleep is common, particularly as a person gets older. Evidence is growing that snoring on a regular basis can make you sleepy during the day and increase your risk for diabetes and heart disease. In addition, some studies link frequent snoring to problem behavior and poorer school achievement in children. Loud, frequent snoring also can be a sign of sleep apnea, a serious sleep disorder that should be evaluated and treated.

Myth 9: Children who don't get enough sleep at night will show signs of sleepiness during the day. Unlike adults, children who don't get enough sleep at night typically become hyperactive, irritable, and inattentive during the day. They also have increased risk of injury and more behavior problems, and their growth rate may be impaired. Sleep debt appears to be quite common during childhood and may be misdiagnosed as attention-deficit hyperactivity disorder.

Myth 10: The main cause of insomnia is worry. Although worry or stress can cause a short bout of insomnia, a persistent inability to fall asleep or stay asleep at night can be caused by a number of other factors. Certain medications and sleep disorders can keep you up at night. Other common causes of insomnia are depression, anxiety disorders, and asthma, arthritis, or other medical conditions with symptoms that tend to be troublesome at night. Some people who have chronic insomnia also appear to be more "revved up" than normal, so it is harder for them to fall asleep. (U.S. Department of Health and Human Services, 2011, p. 22–24)

I end this chapter with some guidelines on avoiding insomnia and improving the overall quality of your sleep. Recognize many of these recommendations are also present in several of the sources already cited in this chapter. When I see multiple authoritative sources with similar or the same guidelines, it gives me increased confidence that I am on the right path. I hope these tips and guidelines in this chapter help you to sleep well and reap the related benefits.

Insomnia and Sleep Health

The following are tips for avoiding insomnia and getting healthy sleep from the NIH U.S. National Library of Medicine-MedlinePlus, updated by Linda J. Vorvick (2018):

People who have insomnia are often worried about getting enough sleep. The more they try to sleep, the more frustrated and upset they get, and the harder it becomes to sleep.

Here are some helpful guidelines to avoid insomnia and improve your quality of sleep:

- While 7 to 8 hours a night is recommended for most people, children and teenagers need more.

- Older people tend to do fine with less sleep at night. But they may still need about 8 hours of sleep over a 24-hour period.
- Remember, the quality of sleep and how rested you feel afterward is as important as how much sleep you get. (Vorvick, 2018)

Change Your Lifestyle

Before you go to bed:

- Write down all the things that worry you in a journal. This way, you can transfer your worries from your mind to paper, leaving your thoughts quieter and better suited for falling asleep. (Vorvick, 2018)

During the day:

- Be more active. Walk or exercise for at least 30 minutes on most days.
- Stop or cut back on smoking and drinking alcohol. And reduce your caffeine intake.
- If you are taking any medicines, diet pills, herbs, or supplements, ask your health care provider about the effects they may have on your sleep.
- Find ways to manage stress.
- Learn about relaxation techniques, such as guided imagery, listening to music, or practicing yoga or meditation.
- Listen to your body when it tells you to slow down or take a break. (Vorvick, 2018)

Change Your Bedtime Habits

- Your bed is for sleeping. DO NOT do things like eat or work while in bed.
- Develop a sleep routine.
- If possible, wake up at the same time each day.
- Go to bed around the same time every day, but not more than 8 hours before you expect to start your day.
- Avoid beverages with caffeine or alcohol in the evening.
- Avoid eating heavy meals at least 2 hours before going to sleep.

- Find calming, relaxing activities to do before bedtime.
- Read or take a bath so that you do not dwell on worrisome issues.
- DO NOT watch TV or use a computer near the time you want to fall asleep.
- Avoid activity that increases your heart rate for the 2 hours before going to bed.
- Make sure your sleep area is quiet, dark, and is at a temperature you like.
- If you cannot fall asleep within 30 minutes, get up and move to another room. Do a quiet activity until you feel sleepy. (Vorvick, 2018)

When to Call the Doctor

Talk to your provider if:

- You are feeling sad or depressed
- Pain or discomfort is keeping you awake
- You are taking any medicine that may be keeping you awake
- You have been taking medicines for sleep without talking to your provider first (Vorvick, 2018)

References:

American Academy of Sleep Medicine. Insomnia - overview and facts. sleepeducation.org/essentials-in-sleep/insomnia. Updated March 4, 2015. Accessed June 14, 2018.

Edinger JD, Leggett MK, Carney CE, Manber R. Psychological and behavioral treatments for insomnia II: implementation and specific populations. In: Kryger M, Roth T, Dement WC, eds. *Principles and Practice of Sleep Medicine.* 6th ed. Philadelphia, PA: Elsevier; 2017: chap 86.

Vaughn BV. Disorders of sleep. In: Goldman L, Schafer AI, eds. *Goldman-Cecil Medicine.* 25th ed. Philadelphia, PA: Elsevier Saunders; 2016:chap 405. (as cited in Vorvick, 2018)

Additionally, "Your Guide to Healthy Sleep" can be downloaded for free: http://www.nhlbi.nih.gov/health/public/sleep/healthy_sleep.htm

Printed copies are available for $3.50 through the NHLBI website or from the NHLBI Information Center at P.O. Box 30105, Bethesda, MD 20824-0105, or at 301-592-8573 or 240-629-3255 (TTY).

Resources to Learn More About Healthy Sleep and Sleep Disorders

- National Center on Sleep Disorders Research: www.nhlbi.nih.gov/sleep
- Sleep, Sleep Disorders, and Biological Rhythms Supplemental Curriculum for Use in High School Biology Classes: http://osedev.od.nih.gov/supplements/nih3/sleep/default.htm.
- Star Sleeper Educational Materials for Children and their Caregivers: http://starsleep.nhlbi.nih.gov

References

Anwar, Y. (2015, June 1). Poor sleep linked to toxic buildup of Alzheimer's protein, memory loss. *Berkeley News.* https://news.berkeley.edu/2015/06/01/alzheimers-protein-memory-loss/

Hamilton, J. (2013, October 17). Brains sweep themselves clean of toxins during sleep. *NPR: All Things Considered.* https://www.npr.org/sections/health-shots/2013/10/18/236211811/brains-sweep-themselves-clean-of-toxins-during-sleep

Maas, J., & Robbins, R. (2010). *Sleep for Success: Everything you must know about sleep but are too tired to ask.* AuthorHouse.

Maas, J., Wherry, M., Axelrod, D., Hogan, B., & Bloomin, J. (1998). *Power sleep: The revolutionary program that prepares your mind for peak performance.* William Morrow Paperbacks.

MedlinePlus. (2018). Changing your sleep habits. In *MedlinePlus: Trusted Health Information for You.* Retrieved May 5, 2020, from https://medlineplus.gov/ency/patientinstructions/000757.htm

National Institutes of Health. (2006, March 23). *NIH offers new comprehensive guide to healthy sleep* [press release]. https://www.nih.gov/news-events/news-releases/nih-offers-new-comprehensive-guide-healthy-sleep

Stone Heart News. (2015, January 8). *Health, Medical, and Science Updates.* http://www.stonehearthnewsletters.com/

U.S. Department of Health and Human Services. (2011). *Your guide to healthy sleep.* https://www.nhlbi.nih.gov/files/docs/public/sleep/healthy_sleep.pdf

Walker, M. (2018). *Why we sleep: Unlocking the power of sleep and dreams.* Scribner.

CHAPTER 6

BUILDING RESILIENCE AND MANAGING STRESS

"It is not length of life, but depth of life."
"Live in the sunshine, swim the sea, drink the wild air."
—Ralph Waldo Emerson, *The Complete Works of Ralph Waldo Emerson*

Chapter Highlights:

- "Looking Good/Feeling Good" Strategies
- Healthy Optimism, Self-efficacy, and Resilience
- Three Cognitive Psychology Tools
- The Power of Music
- Calming Anxiety with Your "Calm Place"
- Mindfulness Helps Tune Your Brain and Nervous System
- Meta-Programs for Building Resilience and Self-Efficacy
- Free Online Course on the Science of Wellbeing
- Three Keys to Increasing Your Joy

Your "Looking Good/Feeling Good" strategies of healthy eating, playfulness, exercise, social support, and quality sleep are five of the top stress coping/resilience building strategies that we know. So, by all means, max out on these five. Keeping track of how these five areas affect your mood and energy is an essential skill to develop and use daily.

Healthy Optimism, Self-Efficacy, and Resilience

These three terms have similar meaning and are very powerful. Martin Seligman coined the term "healthy optimism" and is considered the father of positive psychology. He spent most of his career studying learned helplessness and then turned to explore healthy optimism and authentic happiness. Healthy optimism is the belief in your ability to achieve your goals and not be stopped by temporary setbacks.

"One of the greatest predictors of success is your level of healthy optimistic thinking."
—Martin Seligman (1995)

The core believe is in your ability to succeed. If you lose that belief, you will almost certainly not succeed. So, if you don't doubt your ability, and you are not succeeding, what can you question or doubt? The answer is your strategy. If what you are doing is not working, then change what you are doing, and try a new strategy. If you cannot think of another better strategy, then seek out a helpful person to help your find one. Our optimism cheer:

DON'T DOUBT YOUR ABILITY
DOUBT YOUR STRATEGY
IF WHAT YOU ARE DOING ISN'T WORKING, TRY SOMETHING DIFFERENT

Self-Efficacy

Albert Bandura is famous for his research on self-efficacy. Bandura (1977) defines it as "a person's belief about their ability to reach goals, handle situations, and influence events that effect their lives." A strong sense of self-efficacy enhances your accomplishments and wellbeing. People with high assurance in their capabilities approach difficult tasks as challenges to be mastered rather than threats to be avoided. People with a strong sense of self-efficacy:

- Set challenging goals and maintain strong commitment
- Increase and sustain efforts in the face of failure
- Quickly recover their sense of self-efficacy after a failure or setback
- Attribute failure to insufficient effort or deficient knowledge or skills which are acquirable

Strong self-efficacy produces personal accomplishments, reduces stress, lowers vulnerability to depression, and increases your resiliency. So how do we grow our self-efficacy? The key is having mastery experiences, i.e. experiencing success with challenging tasks. If successes are only around tasks that are easy, we begin to expect quick results and are easily discouraged by failure. The second way of building self-efficacy is observing peers modeling success behaviors, which teaches us new skills and ways of thinking that we can then apply to our own challenges. A third way of building self-efficacy is through social persuasion—being verbally persuaded that we have the capabilities to master the given task. In summary, the best way to build self-efficacy is to structure situations in ways that bring success and avoid placing yourself in situations prematurely where you are likely to fail.

Three Cognitive Psychology Tools

"If we can figure out our non-functional beliefs, we can exchange them for more reasonable ones. This process of corrective self-talk reduces the stress and misery of our lives"
—Kenneth Matheny and Richard Riordan, *Stress and Strategies of Lifestyle Management*
(1992, p. 77)

In addition to the Looking Good/Feeling Good strategies and healthy optimism, try out these three cognitive tools to build your self-efficacy and resilience:

1. Cognitive reframing is one helpful tool for changing how you perceive challenges/ stress. Assume you just made a mistake and your negative self-talk starts in berating you, saying something like: "I can't believe you did that, that's so stupid, you are really losing it." Catch yourself as quickly as possible to cut off this unhelpful tirade and say something like this to yourself instead: "That's not like me to_____ (whatever your mistake was). I'm usually _____ (whatever the fixup would be)." For example, "That's not like me to lose my phone. I'm usually good at knowing where it is."

2. Now if your mind can't accept this reframe because you routinely can't find your phone, then the alternative reframe would be "Up until now____ (the problem) from now on (the fixup)." For example, "Up until now I have had problems keeping up with

my phone, so from now on I will try a new strategy and keep my phone in the same place at home and on me when I leave." The idea is to create, with these two simple reframes, a psychological escape hatch to protect you from destructive negative self-talk that frequently happens when we make mistakes. Believe me, we all will continue to make mistakes, so it helps to has a strategy that limits the damage. Remember: "Don't doubt your ability, doubt your strategy" and "If what you are doing is not working, try something different."

3. Here is one more self-talk strategy that can be a very strong anchor for your wellbeing. "My happiness does not depend on _____."

My challenge to you is to deepen your belief that almost nothing that happens can rob you of your happiness. You can control your reaction to events, and usually, there are alternatives that can put you back into a positive space. I use this for little irritations, such as not making the green light before it turns red (delaying me from being on time for a meeting), to major life setbacks such as the death of a loved one. For serious losses or events, this does not mean avoiding the experience of sadness, mourning, and psychological pain. It rather means you see these as temporary and that your ability to regain your sense of life satisfaction and happiness is still intact. It means that you can almost always choose to be healthy and happy. The one exception I allow to this rule is health. I believe if we lose our health, it may not be possible to maintain life satisfaction and happiness. So, stay serious about taking care of your health and become almost bullet proof.

The Power of Music

As you have no doubt observed, music has the power to affect our moods and energy. Here is a very simple but powerful tool we can use to stay positive and reduce anxiety. Think of a song that, as soon as you hear the first few notes, puts a smile on your face. Now consider creating a special curated playlist—what I call "Keep Kool Tunes"—that can have this effect on you. Next, play these tunes regularly and experience how they positively impact how you feel. Finally, use them as a shield to protect you from negative self-talk when under pressure. We sometimes start negative tapes playing in our mind when under pressure or after making mistakes. For example, "This _____ is way too hard, how do they expect anybody to do this," or "I can't do anything right. I'm never going to get it, everybody will think I'm a loser…"

"Keep Kool Tunes" is a simple technique that you can use to cut this negative message tape off. It involves three easy steps.

"Keep Kool Tunes" Emotional Shield, Your Own Positive Music Shields Against Negative Self-Talk:

1. Pay attention and label what is happening: "Ah-Ha! There's my negative self-talk again!"
2. Start your "Keep Kool Tunes" playing in your head. This will shift you away from your negative message, which robs you of confidence and give you back control of your thinking.
3. Now that you are back in control, decide the best thing to do next.

To use this easy tool, you first have to identify your "Keep Kool Tunes" playlist(s).

Get started making your own custom "Keep Kool Tunes" shield. First, think of at least ten songs that immediately put a smile on your face when you hear them. Next, put these on your favorite listening device (hopefully, one that is mobile, so you can access it wherever you are). Finally, make it a habit to listen to these mood changing songs regularly. This will make it possible for you to play several in your imagination when needed to counter the beginning of any negative self-talk before it brings you down emotionally or increases your anxiety. Everyone's taste in music is different. It does not matter if my "Keep Kool Tunes" playlist works for you, or if your's works for me; what matters is "Do They Work for You?" Do they put a smile on your face whenever you hear them playing (inside or outside of your head)?

Start your "Keep Kool Tunes" playlist here:

1.
2.
3.
4.
5.

6.

7.

8.

9.

10.

Here are a few of my "Keep Kool Tunes":

1. "Do You Believe in Magic?" – Jesse Colin Young
2. "It's a Beautiful Morning" – The Rascals
3. "Blues Skies" – Willie Nelson
4. "It's Alright (to Have a Good Time)" – Curtis Mayfield
5. "I Feel Good" – James Brown
6. "The Happy Song" – Pharrell Williams
7. "The Secret of Life" – James Taylor
8. "Grooving" – The Rascals
9. "Here Comes the Sun" – The Beatles
10. "Upside Down" – Jack Johnson
11. "It Ain't My Fault" – The Brothers Osborne
12. "This Kiss" – Faith Hill
13. "All Day Music" – War
14. "Don't You Worry About It" – John Legend
15. "She Walks This Earth" – Sting

"If we learn to monitor the early buildup of stress, we can prevent its spiraling effects. The key focus should be on the muscles by countering tension with relaxation methods"
—Kenneth Matheny and Richard Riordan, *Stress and Strategies of Lifestyle Management*
(1992, p. 98)

Another strategy for calming ourselves and regaining a sense of control mentally, emotionally, and physically is a relaxation and imagery technique, which I call "Calm Place" (Brigman et al., 2016). It is great for downshifting at bedtime or chilling before giving a talk or any other type of stressful event. Try it out and add it to your toolbox of stress coping skills. Excerpted from Brigman et al. (2016):

Calming Anxiety with Your "Calm Place"

Calm Place

Wouldn't it be great to have a place to go anytime you needed: a place where you felt calm, confident, safe and strong? The good news is anyone can learn to create such a place in your imagination and you can go there anytime you choose

The steps are simple:

First, I will show you how to relax. Then, I will show you how to create your own special "Calm Place" using your imagination. Last, you can start using "Calm Place" right away. For example, when facing a stressful situation, we encourage you to use the "Breathe, Picture, Focus" strategy. First, take a few slow deep breaths. Next, picture yourself in your calm place where you feel calm and confident, strong, and safe. It only takes a few seconds to put you back in charge and reduce the anxiety so that you can focus on the next important task. It is like changing the radio station from loud annoying static to a calming music station. The technical term is incapable response. The calming response you are creating by breathing and picturing yourself in your calm place is incapable with a high anxiety state and so you switch your brain channels to the station you choose.

Note: you may want to record the script below and play it for yourself as you learn to use this simple but powerful technique.

Relaxation:

Sit (or lie) in a comfortable position, with legs and arms uncrossed. Take a few slow deep breaths. Exhale slowly and gently. Let your body go loose and limp like a rag doll. Put your attention on your jaw muscles and tell them to relax and let go. Feel the relaxation spread to your, neck and shoulders. Continue to breath slowly and gently. Allow your back and chest to relax and let go. As you continue to breathe slowly and gently, let this relaxation spread to your stomach and hips. Now, let the muscles in your legs and feet relax deeply. Breathe slowly and gently, and scan your entire body for any tightness. If you find a tight area, place your attention there, and tell that part to relax and let go.

Imagination:

Now, that you are relaxed, I want you to use your imagination to create a special place, your "Calm Place." This is a place where you can feel safe and strong, calm and protected, confident and at ease. This place could be a place you know well, like a room in your home, or a special place you like to go outside, or some place you once visited and loved. Or your calm and confident place could be a combination of these places, or it can also be a totally new place that you create from scratch in your imagination. The important thing is that when you are there in your imagination that you feel calm and confident, safe and strong, protected and at ease.

Take a few moments and create your very special "Calm Place."

In just a moment, I will ask you to return to the room from your "Calm Place" and draw or write something that will help you remember it. Then, you will be able to tell a partner whatever you choose about your "Calm Place."

So, look around your "Calm Place" once more so you can remember as many details as possible. When you are ready, open your eyes, and look around the room.

Draw and Share

Take a few moments and draw something that helps you remember your "Calm Place." We have found that drawing and then sharing your "Calm Place" with someone you are close with are two ways to anchor your "Calm Place" in your mind so that you can use it whenever you choose. We also find that the more your practice going to your "Calm Place," the stronger the calming response, and the quicker you can use it to overcome anxiety.

Mindfulness Helps Tune Your Brain and Nervous System

Mindfulness: A Brief History

Meditation in various forms has been practiced for thousands of years. Herbert Benson, a cardiologist and Professor of Mind/Body Medicine at Harvard Medical School, and Founder of the Mind/body Medical Institute at Massachusetts General Hospital in Boston, was one of the first to study the medical benefits of meditation. Herbert et al. (1976) coined the term, "relaxation response," and studied the physiology of meditation, stripped of religious connotation. His book, *The Relaxation Response*, was first published in 1976. The relaxation response is a secular version of Transcendental Meditation and a precursor to Jon Kabat-Zinn's Mindfulness-based Stress Reduction (MBSR).

In 1979, Kabat-Zinn founded the Mindfulness-Based Stress Reduction program at the University of Massachusetts. MBSR is now widely used in schools, prisons, hospitals, veteran centers and other environments. Kabat-Zinn's research on mindfulness is widely recognized as the greatest force behind the tremendous growth in the use of mindfulness. Kabat-Zinn's MBSR first received attention with his book, *Full Catastrophe Living: Using the Wisdom of Your Body and Mind to Face Stress, Pain, and Illness.* Soon after, his work in the Stress Reduction Clinic was featured in Bill Moyers's PBS special, *Healing and the Mind*, spurring wide interest nationally. In 1994, Kabat-Zinn's second book, *Wherever You Go, There You Are*, became a national bestseller. In the latter part of the 1990s, many MBSR clinics were opened, either as standalone centers or as part of a hospital's holistic medicine program.

Mindfulness: Definition

Mindfulness is moment-by-moment awareness of thoughts, feelings, body sensations, and surrounding environment with acceptance and without judgement. The focus is on what is being sensed rather than ruminations about the past or future. According to Kabat-Zinn (1994), "Mindfulness is paying attention in a particular way: on purpose, in the present moment, and non-judgmentally" (p. 4).

Benefits of Mindfulness

A 2015 systematic review and meta-analysis of randomized controlled trials (RCTs) involving over 8,000 participants, consisting of a wide array of people including different patient categories, as well as healthy adults and children, found evidence supporting the use of mindfulness programs to decrease symptoms of a variety of mental disorders (Gotink et al., 2015). Another meta-analysis on meditation in *JAMA* in 2014, which included over 3,500 participants, concluded there was moderate evidence that meditation reduces anxiety, depression, and pain, but not evidence that meditation was more effective than active treatments such as drugs, exercise, and other behavioral therapies (Goyal et al., 2014).

Meditation: A Daily Workout for Your Brain

Daniel Goleman, PhD, a psychologist known for his work on emotional intelligence, conducted a study of looking at over 6,000 studies on meditation. His team of researchers sought to determine which of the reported benefits had substantial evidence supporting meditation. Goleman co-authored with neuroscientist Richard Davidson, and their findings have been summarized in a book, *Altered Traits: Science Reveals How Mediation Changes Your Mind, Brain, and Body.* Davidson directs a brain lab at the University of Wisconsin-Madison.

Goleman, who wrote his Harvard University dissertation on meditation and stress, found that meditation can decrease depression and anxiety and can boost compassion. Regular meditators can also create lasting positive changes in their brain. The following are summaries from Goleman's research:

Key elements of meditation. Meditation focuses attention and acts as a mental fitness exercise. Meditation involves bringing your attention back to focus when your mind wanders. This process of bringing your attention back to a focus point (your breath, a mantra, an image, a candle) is similar to repetitions of weight-lifting, which strengthens muscle. Meditation strengthens your ability to focus. This repeated practice actually changes the neural circuitry in the brain, and not only makes your ability to focus stronger, but also helps you to be less reactive emotionally to events and thoughts. Repeated studies show many benefits of this practice including: strengthening attention, improving memory, improving learning and regulating your amygdala (the part of the brain responsible for managing your emotional reactions).

Meditation is not about making your mind quiet but bringing your attention back to a point of focus when it wanders. Meditation can help us to be more compassionate. Loving kindness meditation is a technique that has been shown to improve compassion and gratitude. It works by thinking of a person or people who have been kind to you and feeling gratitude for them, along with wishing them well. Next, you think of yourself and feel compassion and gratitude for yourself and send well-wishes. This simple process seems to activate the brain chemical dopamine circuitry associated with wellbeing and strengthens the regulatory circuits that manage stress and lower stress hormones.

How to do it. Goleman presents these tips for beginning meditation:

- Start with your breath. Find a quiet place, sit upright in a comfortable chair, close your eyes and relax. Bring your attention to your breathing. Just notice your natural breathing in and out.

- Notice when your mind wanders and just gently bring it back. Do not judge yourself. Everyone's mind wanders. The idea is to get better at noticing when it begins to wander and not get stuck with the thought. Just bring your attention back to noticing your natural breathing.

- Some people find it helpful to have note paper handy if recurring thoughts pop up. They simply write a few key words down to remind them to pay attention to this topic after meditation. Then, they return to attending to breath.

- Send yourself love. Remember people in your life who have been kind to you and loved you. Focus on feeling that love again from them.

There's an app for it. There are many apps for mindfulness and meditation. For example, "Aura," "Calm," "Headspace," and "iMindfulness," are all well-regarded for those wanting to begin meditating.

Meta-Programs for Building Resilience and Self-Efficacy

Below are four of my favorite meta-programs I use every morning after my mindfulness session to anchor me to a positive mental/emotional state with which to navigate my day. Just as "Keep Kool Tunes" are personalized, these may or may not work for you, but the idea is to create positive self-statements that can help shift our default mental/emotional setting from fear and anxiety about unseen dangers (caveman thinking) to a strong and positive place which can help us build and maintain our sense of resilience and self-efficacy.

1. **PANABHI**

    P   be present
    A   be aware

N	be not attached to outcomes
A	be authentic
B	be balanced in nutrition, fun/playfulness, exercise, social support, and sleep/rest (and enjoy high energy and positive mood as a result)
H	be in harmony with your authentic self, with nature and universal mind and spirit
I	be accepting of deepening inner peace, love, happiness, joy and contentment

2. **Every Day and in Every Way**

"Every day and in every way, I am getting better and better. Negative thoughts and negative suggestions have no influence on me at any level of mind. I will always maintain a healthy body, mind and spirit, and this is so."

3. **Slow Down, Simplify, Focus on the Most Important**

Slow down, simplify, focus on the most important.
Keep your mind and body strong and flexible.
There are always alternatives.
Enjoy your life.

4. **"I Make Good Choices"**

"I make good choices."
"I love and care about myself."
"I love and care about others."
"Others love and care about me."
"I can handle the tasks ahead."
"I am strong and kind."

Free Online Course on the Science of Wellbeing

I recently had a chance to see Laurie Santos, PhD, cognitive psychologist and Professor at Yale University, present an overview of her course on the science of wellbeing. Santos is very engaging, and not only provides very helpful information, but also encourages you to put this new information into practice in your life and provides helpful suggestions about how to do so. Her course was so popular, she decided to offer it free online through Cousera.org. In her course, you will engage in a series of challenges designed to increase your own happiness and build more productive habits. As preparation for these tasks, Santos reveals misconceptions about happiness, annoying features of the mind that lead us to think the way we do, and the research that can help us change. You will ultimately be prepared to successfully incorporate a specific wellness activity into your life. I have taken her online course and highly recommend it. The information reinforces what I have provided in this book and offers other complimentary knowledge and skills you will find useful in your quest to be ridiculously healthy and unreasonably happy.

I will wrap up with "Three Keys for Increasing Your Joy" (see below). This book has presented many ideas that have been shown to increase health and happiness. I encourage you to listen to your inner voice and then choose to put into practice the ideas that seem to be good fits for you. Even if you only regularly apply 1–2 of these ideas, you will find meaningful and long-lasting positive change.

Three Keys to Increasing Your Joy

1. **Do more of what brings you joy and less of what brings you stress.** You do have a choice and the more you allow yourself to say no to the things that bring you down and yes to things that pick you up, the more relaxed and happy you will be.

Increase your fun factor. Turn on some music, do a little dance, or plan a fun get together with your friends. When the going gets tough, go have fun!

Check out your "Things That Bring You Joy" list and put it to work for you. Commit to doing one thing you love every day and say goodbye to stress and hello to bliss.

2. **Practice self-care daily.** Self-care seems to be the first thing to go when we are feeling stressed. Self-care is the time you commit to refilling your cup and refreshing your energy reserves. Your self-care is your plan to do things that clear your mind, energize your body, and feed your soul. Whether it's a run, yoga, meditation, or something else, don't skimp on this time. When you think you don't have time for self-care is the time you need it the most.

Use your Looking Good/Feeling Good chart to track five keys to your healthy self-care.

3. **Invest in your social relationships.** Take time to nurture your most important relationships. The are central to your overall happiness. Both friendships and love relationships need our consistent tending, like a garden needs tending. Make time for connecting with others, enjoying social support and giving social support. Show your concern for the life and growth of others. Practice your ability to be intimate, trusting, self-disclosing with another. Demonstrate your ability to receive & express affection. Increase your capacity for non-possessive caring.

References

Bandura, A. (1977). Self-efficacy: Toward a unifying theory of behavioral change. *Psychological Review, 84*(2), 191–215.

Bandura, A. (1986). *Social foundations of thought and action: A social cognitive theory.* Prentice-Hall.

Bandura, A. (1997). *Self-Efficacy: The exercise of control.* W. H. Freeman.

Benson, H., & Klipper, M. (1976). *The relaxation response.* Avon Books.

Brigman, G., & Webb, L. (2016). *Student success skills.* Atlantic Education Group.

Emerson, R. W. (2015). *The complete works of Ralph Waldo Emerson.* Palala Press.

Goleman, D., & Davidson, R. (2017). *Altered traits: Science reveals how meditation changes your mind, brain, and body.* Avery.

Gotink, R., Chu, P., Busschbach, J., Benson, H., Gregory, F., & Hunink, M. G. (2015). Standardised mindfulness-based interventions in healthcare: An overview of systematic reviews and meta-analyses of RCTs. *PLoS One, 10*(4). http://doi.org/10.1371/journal.pone.0124344

Goyal, M., Singh, S., Sibinga, E. M., Gould, N. F., Rowland-Seymour, A., Sharma, R., Berger, Z., Sleicher, D., Maron, D. D., Shihab, H. M., Ranasinghe, P. D., Linn, S., Saha, S., Bass, E. B., Haythornthwaite, J.A. (2014). Meditation programs for psychological stress and well-being: A systematic review and meta-analysis. *JAMA Intern Med., 174*(3): 357–68. http://doi.org/10.1001/jamainternmed.2013.13018

Kabat-Zinn, J. (1990). *Full catastrophe living: Using the wisdom of your body and mind to face stress, pain, and illness.* Delacorte Press.

Kabat-Zinn, J. (1994). *Wherever you go, there you are: Mindfulness meditation in everyday life.* Hyperion.

Matheny, K., & Riordan, R. (1992). *Stress and strategies for lifestyle management.* Georgia State University Press.

Santos, Laurie. (n.d.). *The science of well-being* [webinar series]. https://www.coursera.org/learn/the-science-of-well-being#reviews

Seligman, M. E. P., Reivich, K., Jaycox, L., & Gillham, J. (1995). *The optimistic child.* Houghton, Mifflin and Company.

Printed in the United States
By Bookmasters